IMAGES
of Sport

TOTTENHAM HOTSPUR
FOOTBALL CLUB
1882-1952

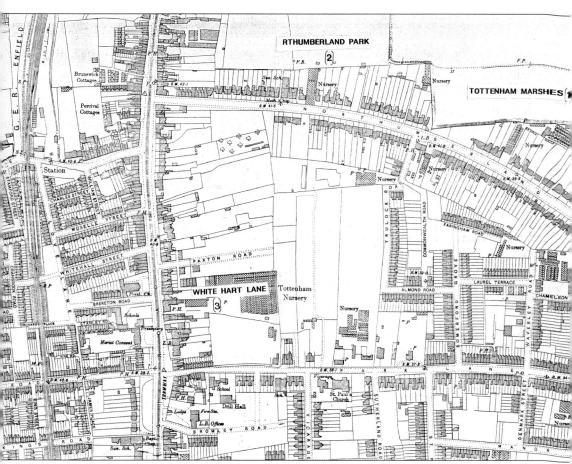

A map of the Tottenham area showing the location of the three grounds that have been used by the club. 'A' is the first ground on Tottenham marshes, 'B' the first enclosed ground in Northumberland Park (now covered by houses) and 'C' the present ground at White Hart Lane, now over 100 years old.

IMAGES
of Sport

TOTTENHAM HOTSPUR
FOOTBALL CLUB
1882-1952

Compiled by
Roy Brazier

TEMPUS

First published 2000, reprinted 2002

Tempus Publishing Limited
The Mill, Brimscombe Port,
Stroud, Gloucestershire, GL5 2QG

British Library Cataloguing in Publication Data.
A catalogue record for this book is available from the British Library.

ISBN 0 7524 2044 5

Typesetting and origination by Tempus Publishing Limited
Printed in Great Britain by Midway Colour Print, Wiltshire

Contents

Acknowledgements

First, I would like to thank Tempus Publishing for approaching me to take on the task of adding Tottenham Hotspur Football Club to their *Images of Sport* series. This is to be produced in two volumes, this one covering 1882 to 1952, and then 1953 to the present day. While I have been a true Tottenham supporter since 1945 and have gathered much about the club in programmes and other items, there are others who have made their collections available for me to view and given permission to use. Nick Manning welcomed me to his home and helped me choose from his large collection, while Alan Rosenthal gave me the benefit of his great knowledge of the club and some precious items to include in this publication. Club historian Andy Porter suggested ways of putting the book together and gave permission to use some of his articles for research, as did Bob Goodwin from his very informative books on the club and its players. Thanks to Tottenham Hotspur themselves who encouraged me in every way when I approached them with the idea, especially John Ireland, and gave permission for some of the photographs to be reproduced in this book. Thanks also to the staff at Bruce Castle Museum at Tottenham for providing some illustrations.

A match in progress at White Hart Lane just after the Second World War.

Introduction

Legend has it that a small band of boys, barely in their teens, gathered under the flickering light from an old street lamp near the junction of Tottenham High Road and Park Lane. They came mainly from St Johns School and Tottenham Grammar School, and lived in the area of Northumberland Park. One thing joined them together, the fact that they were all members of a cricket team who played their matches on Captain Delano's farm, down by the River Lea. Two of the lads were his nephews, so he didn't mind them using part of his land for their summer sport, and they called themselves the Hotspur Cricket Club. These Northumberland Park boys had rivals in a team of boys from the High Road, sons of the local shopkeepers, and it had been heard that they were thinking of forming a football club. The boys who had gathered under the street lamp were discussing this idea as well and thought it would benefit them to play football together during the winter season, as they all wanted to stay as a group. So the Hotspur Football Club, later to add Tottenham to its title, was born from this very modest beginning.

The official date given for the football club's formation was 5 September 1882, this being the day when the first subscriptions were paid in by the initial members. Just eleven lads became the founders of the club: E. Beaven, Bob Buckle (the first captain), Fred Dexter, Stuart Leaman (the first goalkeeper), E. Wall, the Anderson brothers, L. Casey and his brother Sam Casey, and Jack and Peter Thompson. Eight more new members quickly joined the newly created football club, all ready and eager to get going. Jack Jull, who was away at boarding school, was one of the players known as quite useful, and played for the club when he was at home. The Casey brothers' father provided the club with a set of goalposts, which cost two shillings and sixpence, and these were duly painted blue and white. In those far off days the uprights were not joined together by a bar, but by tape. Another Casey brother gave the club its first ball, and they were up and running. The new football club was named 'Hotspur' the same as the cricket club – and you don't have to go far to see why this name was chosen. Tottenham and the surrounding district formed part of the great estates of the Percy family, and Sir Henry Percy was the son of the first Earl of Northumberland and was nicknamed Harry Hotspur. He had a reputation as a bold and courageous warrior. The place to play gave no problems, with the wide expanses of Tottenham Marshes nearby. This area was free, they just had to go along and mark out a pitch and erect the posts. The lads favoured the northern end of the marshes, with the Great Eastern Railway line close to one of the touchlines.

As newcomers, the Hotspur boys often came up against trouble, and sometimes their carefully marked pitch was taken over by other teams with bigger lads in their midst, so the new team looked for more adult help for their second season in existence. It was through the father of the Thompson brothers, who was a churchwarden at All Hallows church in Tottenham, that Mr John Ripsher, a bible teacher, was approached and he quickly agreed to hold a meeting at the YMCA premises at Percy House in the High Road. He became the first president of the club and started it off on a firm footing. Rules were drawn up, an interesting one being that the colours were to be navy blue with a red shield bearing the letter 'H'. In 1884/85 the side officially became Tottenham Hotspur Football Club. Only friendly matches were played at first with odd incidents abounding. A match versus Brownlow Rovers was abandoned due to the ball bursting, at times the club played with less than eleven players, and on occasions only sixty or seventy minutes were played.

After three seasons of friendlies they took part in their first competitive match against St Albans, who were also a London club, in the London FA Cup and it was estimated that 400 spectators saw Tottenham win 5-2. However, they lost 8-0 to the Casuals at Wandsworth in the next round. The club then decided to change their colours to blue and white halves after watching Blackburn Rovers in the FA Cup final at The Oval. During this season they moved their headquarters to Dorset Villas in Northumberland Park, again with the help of their president, Mr Ripsher, but on condition they attended church each Wednesday. Their dressing rooms were at the 'Milford' in Park Lane, from where they had to walk about a mile to the ground. They were becoming a club of note in the area – lots of players were wanting to join from other clubs – and they were attracting large crowds to the marshes.

For their seventh season, Tottenham Hotspur moved to an enclosed ground in Northumberland Park and this was their ground when they entered the Southern League in 1896. They had turned professional after an incident, when they gave a new player some money to go and buy a pair of boots after he had turned up without any – they were locked up at his former club's headquarters. Tottenham were then still an amateur club, and after being punished for this offence decided to encompass professionalism. They joined the Football Association in 1888 with a balance of £6 in hand. The colours were chocolate and gold for a while before the familiar white shirts seen today were decided upon, after the famous Preston North End team of that period.

Tottenham won the championship of the Southern League in 1899/1900 and the FA Cup in 1901 when still a non-League club – a feat that has not been accomplished since (and probably never will be). Crowds of up to 15,000 were attending Northumberland Park, so the club moved to White Hart Lane in 1899 – they have recently celebrated their centenary at the stadium. At a meeting on 2 March 1898 the new Tottenham Hotspur Football and Athletic Company was formed with 8,000 shares offered to the public at £1 each. In 1908 they gained admission to the Football League and were placed in Division Two, from which they promptly gained promotion to the top division in their first season. They remained there until the First World War when they dropped into the Second Division for the restart of League Football in 1920. Again they won promotion at the first attempt and went on to win the FA Cup again in 1921 – the 'year ending in one' was beginning to have quite an effect already! Eight years with the top teams followed before losing their place in 1927/28, and it was another five years before they regained Division One status again in 1933. This was to be their briefest stay as they were relegated after only two years. They did not regain top-flight football until 1950, when they won the Second Division in great style, before going on to even greater glories in 1951 when they were champions of Division One for the first time.

Tottenham have always been noted as a skilful side and have never given up this style of play, although the playing personnel change over the years – it is said you have to be something special to play for the Spurs. From Bobby Buckle in the early years, through John Cameron, V. J. Woodward, Arthur Grimsdell, Jimmy Dimmock, Willie Evans and Willie Hall, to Ted Ditchburn and Ron Burgess in the seasons following the Second World War, the white shirts of Tottenham were worn by some of the most skilful players of their day.

One

In the Beginning

Probably the earliest photograph of Tottenham Hotspur Football Club, this was taken in 1884/85. The group includes several founder members of the club from 1882. From left to right, back row: L. Brown, T. Wood, T. Bumberry, J. Anderson, J. Ripsher (president), H. D. Casey. Middle row: W. Amos, W. Tyrell, F. Lovis, J. Jull, H. Goshawk, H. Hillyer, S. Leaman, A. Bayne, J. Randall. Front row: J. Thompson Jnr, W. Randall, R. Buckle, G. Burt, G. Bush, P. Moss, W. Mason, W. Harston, F. Cottrell, H. Bull. The team were playing on Tottenham marshes at this time and using dressing room accommodation in Somerford Grove, off Park Lane. They are wearing their light blue and white halved shirts, which they adopted after watching Blackburn Rovers play Queens Park in the FA Cup final at the Kennington Oval. W. Harston was probably the most long-standing link with the original team, as he was still with the club into the 1940s, being doorman to the press box – this after being bombed out of his home during the war.

Bobby Buckle was one of the founder members of Tottenham Hotspur and the first elected captain, when aged about fourteen. He served on the committee from 1884, was secretary and treasurer in 1890 and on the first board of directors in 1898. Buckle worked as a solicitor's clerk in the City and continued to play until 1895, but when he married in 1901 he moved from his native Tottenham to Surrey, where he died in 1959, aged ninety.

A page from the original minute book for the Tottenham Hotspur Football Club, dated Wednesday 29 April 1885. It is interesting to note that the stationmaster at the Park Railway Station (now Northumberland Park) was given a present for looking after the poles for the goalposts for the team. The president Mr Ripsher had been very generous in his help to the young club.

The Third Annual General Meeting of The Tottenham-Hotspur Football Club, was held at the "Red House" on Wednesday the 29th April 1885 at 8.30pm.

J. Ripsher Esqre in the Chair.

The Secretary (Mr H D Bang) being absent the Report was read by Mr Mason which read as follow:- 1st. Matches played 24, won 10 lost and 10 drawn. 82 Goals won and 34 lost.

1st eleven played 30, won 18, lost 5, drew 5, scratched 2.

Seconds eleven played 16; won 6, lost 5, drew 5 scratched 13.

The Treasurer (J Ripsher Esqre) then read his Statement which showed that £5.0.1. had been received and £4.11.1 expended leaving a balance of 9/- which was to be partly expended in printing a Report of the progress of the Club with a view of getting Honorary Members.

It was then resolved that a present should be made by voluntary contributions to Mr Hardin the Station Master at Park for his kindness in taking charge of the poles &c. A hearty vote of thanks was proposed by Mr Hanson to Mr Ripsher (with great cheering) for the funds away in which he had helped the Club financially & otherwise & also for the tea he had provided that evening. He said in reply that it was a great pleasure to him to be able to help the Club in any way & he thought that the Club had on the whole a very successful season. They had it was true suffered more defeats than last season, but that he was sure was owing to the strong Clubs they had played in fact that had sometimes been looked upon with contempt by Clubs who came down to play them owing to their size, but he was glad to say that the Tottenham Hotspur generally managed to give a good account of themselves.

A BALANCE OF NINE-SHILLINGS

On being asked to leave their premises at the local YMCA, Spurs were able to use the upper part of the Red House Coffee Palace at 748 Tottenham High Road, which is seen here. The young players were provided with various games and a library, together with refreshments. The building was operating as the Red House Hotel when Spurs moved to their present ground at White Hart Lane, just behind the hotel, at the turn of the century. The club acquired the hotel property in 1921 and used it as their offices, and in 1934 fixed the clock to the front and surmounted it with the figure of a cockerel soon after. It was not until 1937 that the club's official address was moved to the Red House from 750 High Road, the number of the White Hart public house. The Spurs continue to use the premises for various activities up to the present day.

THE

Tottenham ♦ Hotspur

FOOTBALL CLUB.

✦ SEASON ✦ 1895-1896. ✦

One of the earliest season tickets, from when Tottenham were still playing at the Northumberland Park ground.

The Tottenham Hotspur line-up for 1894/95. The colours had now changed to red shirts with blue shorts and their nickname became 'The Reds'. Top left: the Briggs brothers. From left to right, third row: Petter, Campbell, Hurry, Williams, Baldock, Smith, T. Jull, Leaman, Walford, Allen, J. Jull Jnr, Godfrey, Bullock, Norris, Monk, Thompson, J. Jull Snr, Dexter. Second row: Casey, Baxter, Bull, Oliver, Buckle. Front row: Mason, Logan, Harston. Spurs were now playing at Northumberland Park, having moved to their private ground, situated on the north side between numbers 69 and 75, in 1888. This ground was in a meadow behind a nursery, and large enough to share another pitch with the Foxes Football Club and a tennis club, the rent being £10 per season. The Tottenham club had made a profit of £6 after one season there. The club entered the FA Cup for the first time in 1894, but after winning through the first three qualifying matches, went out to Luton Town after a replay. Eight games were played in the FA Amateur Cup before losing out to Old Carthusians 5-0 – although they beat the same team 5-1 two weeks later in a friendly fixture. Spurs began to travel a little further for friendlies at Southampton and Bristol, and also entertained visitors from the north, notably Liverpool and Sheffield. A significant arrival at Tottenham in 1894 was Mr John Oliver, who became president when John Ripsher stood down. Oliver ran a carpet factory in Old Street, where some of the players worked, and he was very interested in the club. It was he who paid for a stand to be built at Northumberland Park and, although the club was in debt at this time, he was prepared to advance cash to help them.

The Tottenham 1896 eleven who lined up for their first home match in their initial season as a professional club in the Southern League. They lost this match to Chatham 3-2. From left to right, back row: J. Campbell, H.D. Casey, J. Devlin, L. Burrows, Stanley Briggs, C. Ambler, W. Crump, F. King, J. Montgomery, R. Bullock. Front row: R. McEihaney, J. Milliken, W. Newbigging, R. Clement, E. Payne. In February, Jock Montgomery became the first Spurs player to represent the Southern League in a Southern League XI v. London FA XI fixture at Catford. Their were three Spurs amateurs in the London side and the match ended as a 3-3 draw. The club's secretary Ralph Bullock resigned during the season and H.D. 'Sam' Casey took over. Bullock had a long association with Tottenham, before emigrating to the USA in 1902, and when he came back to join the club again he was Commander Ralph Bullock CBE. He served as an auditor until his death in 1946. Ernie Payne had unwittingly become the reason for Tottenham becoming a professional club when he turned up for his first game with no outfit in 1893. After kitting him out, Spurs could not find any boots so they gave him ten shillings to go and buy a pair. This proved their undoing and the club were found guilty of professionalism and suspended for a fortnight. They went on to became fully professional in 1895. In their first Southern League season they finished fourth, and eighth in the United League and, worryingly, a loss of £500 was entailed off the field. Only seven players of the thirty-two who had played were retained at the end of the season, so committee members Buckle and Bullock went on a scouting mission which resulted in eleven more professionals, mainly from the north, being signed for the following campaign.

Action from the FA Cup-tie between Tottenham and Newton Heath (later to become Manchester United) at Spurs' Northumberland Park ground, in January 1899 in front of 13,721 spectators. The match ended in a 1-1 draw but Spurs won the replay 5-3 at Clayton, after being 3-1 behind. James McNaught, who scored one of the goals, had joined Spurs from Newton Heath the year before. Tottenham were the last side to play at Manchester United's Clayton ground in January 1910 – it was to have been the first match at their new Old Trafford ground, but arrangements were put back a week. Ten FA Cup matches were played by Spurs in 1899, but they only reached the third round, replays having been necessary on the way. Tottenham had entered three leagues for the 1898/99 season: the Southern League, the United League and the Thames & Medway League. They finished in third position in all three. It was also the year when they played their first benefit game for one of their players, William Joyce, who was Spurs' leading scorer for the two seasons he was with the club. In 1897 he notched up 54 goals and the next year 38 – a grand total of 92 in 119 appearances – before he moved on to Thames Ironworks. Joyce also scored twice for the United League v. Thames & Medway League held at Northumberland Park in 1898, one of the first representative matches on a Spurs ground.

Action from the first match at White Hart Lane in 1899. A crowd of 5,000 turned out to see the Tottenham friendly against Notts County, which marked the opening of the new ground in the High Road. Several names were put forward for this prodigious new ground, amongst them 'Percy Park' and 'Gilpin Park', but nothing official was decided and the ground soon earned its own natural name of White Hart Lane. Most of the stands from the Northumberland Park ground were re-erected at the new ground. After the ceremonial kick off by Mr Roberts, the Spurs chairman, Notts County, the oldest League club, were defeated by 4-1.

The Spurs side consisted of: Crawley, Erentz, Tait, Jones, McNaught (captain), Morris, Smith, Pratt, Copeland, Cameron and Kirwan – there was not a Londoner among them. David Copeland scored a hat-trick.

A Tottenham Hotspur match at the beginning of the twentieth century – one of the early games at the new White Hart Lane ground. The identity of the opponents is not known, but it is most likely to be a Southern League match.

Stanley Briggs, seen here in Clapton's colours, was one of the top amateur footballers of his time, and a member of Tottenham's side on many occasions between 1891 and 1898. Born locally, he was playing for Folkstone at the age of fourteen, while at school in the seaside town. As an amateur he could play for any club, but Spurs were always his first love, and when they embraced professionalism, he only spent one more season with them before playing regularly with Clapton.

Two

A New Century

The Tottenham team of 1899/1900. From left to right, back row: J.L. Jones, H. Erentz, J. Melia, G. Clawley, A. Tait, D. Copeland. Middle row: W. Johnson (trainer), C.D. Roberts (chairman), R. Stormont, J. McNaught, T. Morris, E. Hughes, T.A. Deacock (director), C. Taylor (assistant trainer). Front row: T. Smith, T. Pratt, J. Cameron (secretary), J. Raby, L. Hyde, J. Kirwain. Tottenham won the Southern League championship in this first season at White Hart Lane. The old ground at Northumberland Park had been deemed unsafe for the crowds they were attracting, and the final straw had been when a stand roof collapsed at the Woolwich Arsenal match on Good Friday 1899. The team had spent eleven years at the old ground.

Tottenham's 1901 FA Cup winning team (the only non-League side to achieve this honour) were playing in the Southern League at the time. From left to right, back row: C. Taylor (assistant trainer), Harry Erentz, George Clawley, Sandy Tait, W. Johnson (trainer). Middle row: John Cameron, Tom Morris, Ted Hughes, Jack Jones, John Kirwin. Front row: Tom Smith, Sandy Brown, David Copeland. Spurs were the underdogs for the final, their opponents Sheffield United having no fewer than nine international players in their side, not to mention the giant figure of William Foulkes between the posts. Sheffield had tasted success in the FA Cup by winning the trophy two years previously in 1899. United took the lead, but two goals from Brown put Spurs in front, only for the Blades to level with a disputed equalizer. Spurs goalkeeper Clawley had juggled with the ball before conceding a corner kick, only for referee Mr Kingscott to rule it had crossed the line, thus awarding a goal to Sheffield. The large crowd had nearly prevented the match taking place, as when the Spurs team arrived at the main gate to find a mass of people blocking the way, they were moved to a private entrance to get in. When they were told to go back to the main gate, Mr Bullock, who was in charge of the Spurs party, sent a message to the FA officials saying they would have to take the blame if the match was not played – this did the trick and they were quickly escorted into the stadium.

The programme for the Tottenham Hotspur v. Sheffield United FA Cup final at Crystal Palace on Saturday 20 April 1901, when Spurs brought the trophy back to the south again, after a lapse of nearly twenty years. The last southern team to win it had been the Old Etonians in 1882. A historic record crowd of officially 114,815 (but probably many more), gathered at the Crystal Palace to see the north against south battle, which ended all square and needed a replay the following week at Burnden Park, Bolton.

CRYSTAL PALACE.

Final Tie for the Football Association Challenge Cup.
TOTTENHAM HOTSPUR v. SHEFFIELD UNITED.

Saturday, April 20th. **Kick-off 3.30 p.m.**

WHITE SHIRTS. **TOTTENHAM HOTSPUR.**

RIGHT.

Goal.
x
CLAWLEY

Backs.
x   x
ERENTZ   TAIT

Half-Backs.
x   x   x
MORRIS   HUGHES   JONES

Forwards.
x   x   x   x   x
SMITH   CAMERON   BROWN   COPELAND   KIRWAN

O

Forwards.
x   x   x   x   x
LIPSHAM   PRIEST   HEDLEY   FIELD   BENNETT

Half-Backs.
x   x   x
NEEDHAM   MORREN   JOHNSON

Backs.
x   x
BOYLE   THICKETT

Goal.
x
FOULKES

LEFT.

RIGHT.

LEFT.

SHEFFIELD UNITED.   RED & WHITE SHIRTS.

Referee—Mr. A. KINGSCOTT (Derby).
Linesmen—Messrs. C. SQUIRES (London) and A. J. HINES (Nottingham).

The football ground at the old Crystal Palace, where the FA Cup final was contested from 1895 until 1914. This photograph shows the glass crystal palace towering in the background.

Tottenham's centre forward, Sandy Brown, is shown scoring Spurs' second goal, from a pass from John Cameron. This action shot also gives a good view of the vast crowd at the 1901 Cup Final, with many spectators taking to the trees to get a better, if not slightly precarious, vantage point. Crystal Palace was not the ideal place for a football match as the ground was oval shaped and many spectators were quite a long way from the play.

Alexander 'Sandy' Brown, Tottenham's leading scorer when they won the cup in 1901, netted in every round of the competition, including all four goals in the 4-0 victory over West Bromwich Albion in the semi-final and a hat-trick at Preston in an earlier round. Brown was only at Tottenham for two seasons, but scored 60 in 79 appearances. Coming to Spurs from Portsmouth, he returned to his former club in 1902. In spite of his ability to find the net consistently, he represented his native Scotland on just a single occasion.

Action from the 1901 Cup Final replay at Bolton which Spurs won 3-1, surmounting the anguish of the goal-that-wasn't the week before. A small crowd of just over 20,000 saw Spurs outplay Sheffield on a cold and wet day. Tottenham High Road was packed that evening, although the train bringing the victorious team was not due in London until after midnight, reaching North London around 2.00 a.m. It was dawn before the streets were quiet again, and the newspapers were proclaiming 'Hail Hotspur, Champions of England'.

Tottenham Hotspur Football Club, Limited.

HOTSPUR v SHEFFIELD CUP-TIE MATCHES.

ANIMATED PICTURES

Of the above Matches, shewing the play at the Crystal Palace and at Bolton,

WILL BE GIVEN ON THE

SPURS' FOOTBALL GROUND,

MONDAY EVENING, APRIL 29th.

Many other pictures of local interest will also be shewn by the Prestwich Manufacturing Company, of Tottenham.

TOTTENHAM BRASS BAND
WILL BE IN ATTENDANCE.

ADMISSION, 6d.   BOYS, 3d.

GATES OPEN 8 P.M.   PICTURES 9 P.M.

IF the Spurs Win the Cup, a grand
DISPLAY OF FIREWORKS
WILL CONCLUDE THE ENTERTAINMENT.

JOHN CAMERON, Secretary,
High-road, Tottenham.

An announcement in the local press advertising films of the two matches which brought the cup to Tottenham. The celebrations had hardly wound down before 12,000 turned up for this showing, which was projected on to a large sheet hung up in front of the grandstand. Under a bright moon, there was more singing, music and dancing, and the cup was on view to everyone. The film also showed that the disputed goal in the first match had, in fact, never crossed the line.

Tottenham had surprised everyone when they secured the transfer of J.L. 'Jack' Jones from Sheffield United in 1897, as he was Wales first choice left half and Spurs were still in the Southern League. He was captain of Spurs when they lifted the FA Cup. One of the most skilful players of his day, he won 21 Welsh caps during his career, 12 while at Tottenham. He stayed with Spurs until 1904.

One of the most inspired signings for Tottenham in the early days was that of John Cameron in 1898, and he was appointed secretary-manager as well as being a player. He was also secretary of the Players and Trainers Union. Cameron built the sides that won the Southern League and the FA Cup for Tottenham, his team consisting of five Scotsmen, three Englishmen, two Welshmen and one Irishman. He was coaching in Germany when the First World War started and was interned, returning to England after the war to become a football journalist.

A Tottenham v. Millwall encounter in 1903, when both sides were in the Southern League, the visitors winning this match 1-0. This photograph, taken from the west stand, shows play at the Park Lane end, and a good view of the small east stand and terrace – which was not fully covered at this time. Tottenham were still competing in three leagues and had a good season, with second place being attained in the Southern and London Leagues and first place in the Western League. They also reached the quarter-finals of the FA Cup before going out to Sheffield Wednesday. It was in this season that the FA Cup match at home to Aston Villa in the third round had to be abandoned when the crowd invaded the pitch. Spurs had put in extra seating around the stadium in readiness for the big crowd that was expected, and when the people in these seats decided to stretch their legs at half-time, others followed and spilled onto the pitch. Tottenham, who were 1-0 down at the time, were fined £50 and the match was replayed at Villa Park, when Spurs proceeded to win by the only goal from John 'Bristol' Jones.

"COULD YOU TELL ME THE WAY TO THE
'HOTSPURS' GROUND, PLEASE."

A cartoon from the Tottenham Hotspur handbook for 1903/04 entitled 'Could you tell me the way to the Hotspur's ground please?' This is passing comment on the big crowds seen in the High Road on Spurs' match days.

On Monday 6 April 1903, Tottenham entertained the renowned Scottish club Queens Park for a friendly match at White Hart Lane, the Spurs side consisting mainly of reserve players, although John Cameron played at centre forward. This is a verse penned in greeting to the Queens Park club on their first visit.

LONDON'S GREETING
TO THE
Famous "Queen's Park," Glasgow
On their visit to Tottenham, April 6th, 1903.

From Bonnie Scotland, here they come,
Good men of high renown,
From Bonnie Scotland, here they come
To take the Hotspur down.

Chorus—
Yet not one "brave" who fights but fails,
Will either fret or whine,
They meet as foes, but part as friends,
For "Auld Lang Syne."

Each sturdy youth's well primed with grit,
A grit that baffles fate,
As bright as Copeland, and as fit
As genial Sandy Tate.

Chorus—

Their comrades strove and conquer'd too,
In Sheffield's busy town,
We give the gallant clan their due,
That took Old England down.

Chorus—

Right valiantly the rivals fought,
Fought squarely man to man,
And Woodward sent in number one,
As only Woodward can.

Chorus—

Jack Kirwan spent eight years at Tottenham from 1899 to 1907, after coming from his native Ireland to play for Southport and Everton. Spurs manager John Cameron, also from Everton, brought him to Spurs when he moved to the club. Although rather small and light, he kept quite free from injury and was a fixture at outside left in the early twentieth century. He was also a regular for the Ireland side, winning 12 caps while at Tottenham and more after he moved on. When Chelsea were formed, Kirwan and his wing partner Copland moved across to West London to join them. Altogether he made 345 appearances for Spurs and was the scorer of 97 goals. It was John Kirwan who snatched up the match ball at the end of the 1901 Cup Final and kept it until his death in 1959.

A view of Tottenham High Road, 1905, with the football crowds swarming out of White Hart Lane at the final whistle. An interesting feature is the lack of public transport: only one horse-drawn waggonette can be seen, most people apparently preferring to walk. The main entrance to the ground is near the white building in the distance on the right. The photograph was taken from the roof of Hunnings the printers at 516 High Road.

PROMINENT FOOTBALLERS.

W. BULL,

TOTTENHAM HOTSPUR.

Walter Bull signed for Tottenham in 1904 after eight years with his home club Notts County, where he had gained a good reputation in the game. Although he had played in many different positions, he was noted as a half-back and, after a dispute over the transfer fee, Spurs had to part with £300 for his services. Off the field he was a committee member of the newly formed Players Union. After leaving Spurs in 1909 he had a spell coaching in Argentina, having toured there with Tottenham a few years before.

Scotsman Peter Kyle had a reputation as a colourful character when Tottenham signed him in 1905, and he impressed with a goal in each of his first four games for the club. He linked well with V.J. Woodward and looked to be a valuable member of the team, but in between matches in March 1906 he was, together with another player, suspended for a serious breach of the training rules and neither of the two put on a Spurs shirt again.

Goalkeeper John Eggett, who was born in Wisbech, came via West Ham to Tottenham, after making his name at Doncaster Rovers. He also had half a season at Woolwich Arsenal in between. After making his Spurs debut in October 1904, he became a regular between the posts until an injury let in newly signed 'keeper Reilly and Eggett was unable to regain his position. He left Tottenham for Croydon Common in April 1907.

One of the earliest meetings of Woolwich Arsenal and Tottenham at Plumstead in 1906, the occasion being the semi-final replay of the Southern Charity Cup. Spurs lost the game 5-0 after a goalless draw in the first match. Tottenham goalkeeper Eggett is clearing from the Arsenal forwards in this photograph. The first ever meeting of these two clubs had been on 19 November 1887 at Tottenham marshes, when the match was abandoned with fifteen minutes to go, due to poor light, with Spurs leading 2-1. That initial match had been during Spurs' last season on the marshes, as they were having to erect stakes and ropes around their pitch, as large crowds (reported to be in the region of 4,000) were turning up to see their games. An interesting incident occurred when both sides met in a Southern District Combination match at Woolwich Arsenal on 24 April 1900, the game being abandoned because of 'bad language' – and this from the small attendance of only 500 in the Manor Field, which was Arsenal's home ground for just two seasons (using military wagons as temporary grandstands). Arsenal's top manager Herbert Chapman was a player with Tottenham between 1904 and 1907 and the two sides were bitter rivals even before the Arsenal moved to Highbury in North London.

In 1906 an attempt was made to popularize baseball, the national game of the United States of America, in England during the summer months. The venture met with a fair amount of success for a while and Tottenham were one of the soccer clubs to give this a try out. Eight home matches were played at White Hart Lane including the semi-final of the British Baseball Cup, won 17-2 against Woolwich, and the final versus the Nondescripts, which resulted in a 16-5 victory for Tottenham. Pictured are the Spurs and the Nondescripts, who played their home games on the Ilford football ground at Newbury Park, before the final at White Hart Lane, which drew 4,000 spectators. Amongst the players shown can be seen Tottenham old-timers John Cameron (sitting at the far left of the front row), Tom Morris (standing at the far left of the middle row wearing a cap) and John Over (two places to the right of Over in the lower row of standing players). Note the original grandstand to the left of the picture and the houses in Paxton Road, now obscured from view by the North Stand. Two baseball teams were run the next summer by Tottenham and season tickets were issued at five shillings, this covering thirteen fixtures. The British Baseball Cup was again won by Spurs in 1908, by beating the host side at Leyton 8-6. The last baseball game at Tottenham was on 8 August, just a few weeks before the Spurs' opening football match in the Football League.

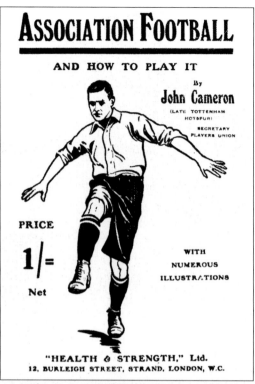

ASSOCIATION FOOTBALL

AND HOW TO PLAY IT

By

John Cameron

(LATE TOTTENHAM HOTSPUR)

SECRETARY PLAYERS UNION

PRICE

1/=

Net

WITH
NUMEROUS
ILLUSTRATIONS

"HEALTH & STRENGTH," Ltd.
12, BURLEIGH STREET, STRAND, LONDON, W.C.

An interesting book written by John Cameron in 1907, introducing the idea of how football should be played. Not just an instruction manual, he deals with many other subjects, showing his own refined way of writing in an era in which footballers were not looked upon as any sort of journalists.

This Tottenham team photograph was taken before an FA Cup-tie against Hull City in 1907. The team was: Reilly, Watson, Tait, Morris, Bull, Hughes, Walton, Hewitt, V. Woodward, Reid and Brearley. The first match produced no goals, so the replay was at Hull the following Thursday, the Spurs players preparing for the match at Withernsea. The supporters were offered a special rail fare of eleven shillings return from Finsbury Park to Hull. Again there were no goals and the match was halted in extra time, due to the fading light. In the third game Herbert Chapman scored the winning goal for Spurs; he had taken the place of Woodward.

When the move from Northumberland Park to White Hart Lane was made in 1899, all the old stands were moved to the new ground as they were. There were seats under cover for 2,500 spectators, and provision made for the parking of bicycles and stabling for horses. Seen here is the back of the old stands in 1908, awaiting much needed reconstruction.

The 1908/09 Tottenham Hotspur line-up for the club's first season in the Football League. From left to right, back row: T. Deacock (director), Walton, Morris, Minter, Hewitson, Burton, Coquet, M. Cadman (director), Nie (trainer). Front row: R. Steele, Woodward, D. Steele, Middlemiss, Darnell. A few weeks prior to the start of the season, the club had faced the prospect of filling the coming campaign with a series of friendly games. They had already resigned from the Southern League, but had initially not received enough votes to gain election to the Football League, and it was only through a last minute decision by Stoke to withdraw from the League that Spurs took their place in Division Two by a casting vote.

Vivian Woodward, often said to be the best centre forward that Tottenham Hotspur ever had, remained an amateur all through his career, playing 67 times for the England Amateurs and captaining the United Kingdom side which won the Olympics in 1908 and 1912. He was also selected for the full England team 23 times, scoring 28 goals – an exceptional average. He appeared in a Spurs shirt for the first time in 1901, but business commitments kept his appearances down at first. However, by 1909 he had played 197 games and had 100 goals to his name. It is worth beaing in mind that this was at a time when the centre forward position was, more often than not, filled by a hard, bustling type of player, whereas Woodward relied on pure skill and touch. He was an all-round sportsman, being a useful cricketer and tennis player, and was even a director of Tottenham for one year (1908/09). His conduct was such that other players, and even some officials, called him 'Sir'. Woodward had started his soccer career while attending college at Clacton, and played for that town's team, also appearing for Harwich and Parkeston before turning out for Chelmsford City. It was in 1909 that he decided to step down from the top level and again play for Chelmsford, but soon appeared in the First Division once again, this time with Chelsea, with whom he remained until the First World War when he joined the army. Woodward retired from football during the conflict.

With such a romantic name as Tottenham Hotspur, the club brought out the best in most things. One of the most intriguing being this piece of music entitled *The Football Match* and dedicated to Tottenham 'in admiration of their many gallant games'. It was written in 1908 as a tribute to their leaving the Southern League for the Football League.

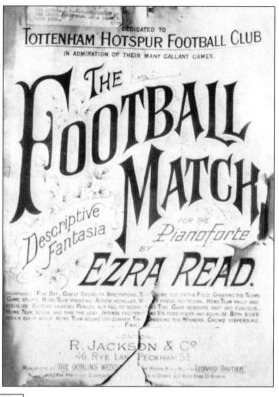

On tour in Argentina, Tottenham and Everton met twice in South America in 1909, the first time professional clubs had been to that country. This programme was for their second meeting in Palermo on 19 June 1909 when Everton won 4-0.

The Tottenham party ready to leave for their tour of Argentina and Uruguay in June 1909. Mr Charles Roberts, the club chairman, is second from the right. They had been invited to South America after winning promotion to Division One in their first season in the Football League. On the tour they crowded seven matches into nineteen days and all the games versus South American opposition were won, with a goal record of 26 scored and only a single goal conceded. This tour was probably a high spot for goalkeeper Fred Boreham, who kept goal for all the Spurs games on the trip, although he only appeared in 20 League matches for Tottenham. Boreham returned to his former club Leyton in 1910. The Spurs team were surprised when watching a local game, when some cavalry troops rode onto the pitch, but were told it was their way of stopping people trying to get in when the ground was full. Some rifle shots also worried them when they were out on the town, so they beat a hasty retreat, to be told the next day that several people had been shot in the street. A fancy dress party on the ship travelling home saw two players dress as Robinson Crusoe and Man Friday, complete with a real parrot. The bird was brought back to Tottenham and was said to have died the day Spurs failed to gain re-election to Division One in 1919.

A view of the ground in 1909, showing the east side and the low stand which had been built to cover part of the terracing. Advertising boards were numerous at this time but were later removed, not returning to White Hart Lane for a long period. A massive crowd of 40,000 squeezed into the ground for the game against Oldham Athletic on Boxing Day 1908.

Robert Steel, the brother of Daniel, was an inside forward with Tottenham between 1908 and 1916, when he gave up playing. He took up refereeing for a while before making a comeback with Gillingham. In his latter days he played bowls and captained the England team. Another brother, Alex, was also with Spurs, but only once were all three in the same Spurs team, for the match against Bradford City at home on 29 January 1909.

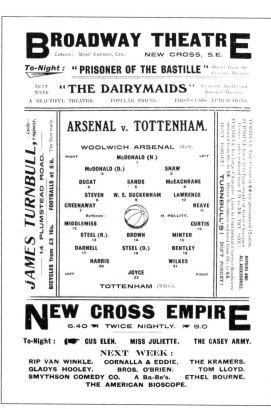

ARSENAL v. TOTTENHAM.

WOOLWICH ARSENAL (Red).

RIGHT   McDONALD (H.)   LEFT
1

McDONALD (D.)   SHAW
2   3

DUCAT   SANDS   McEACHRANE
4   5   6

STEVEN   W. E. BUCKENHAM   LAWRENCE
8   9   10

GREENAWAY   NEAVE
7   11

Referee —   H. POLLITT.

MIDDLEMISS   CURTIS
12   15

STEEL (R.)   BROWN   MINTER
13   14   15

DARNELL   STEEL (D.)   BENTLEY
17   16   19

HARRIS   WILKES
20   21

LEFT   JOYCE   RIGHT
22

TOTTENHAM (White).

The programme for the first League meeting between Woolwich Arsenal and Tottenham on 4 December 1909. On the same day the reserve teams of the two clubs were meeting at Tottenham in the South Eastern League. 'Tiny' Joyce was playing his second game in goal for Tottenham after moving from Millwall a few weeks previously. 'Tiny' scored two goals for Spurs, one in a League match against Bolton Wanderers on 10 April 1914 and another when on tour versus Bayern Munich in May 1914, from the penalty spot. It was on this tour that he received a head wound from an umbrella strike by a wrathful fan in one violent match.

A leisurely training session in 1909 with, from left to right: Wood, McFarlane, Payne, Gipps and Massey. Doug McFarlane was at centre forward for Spurs' first Football League match, George Payne was badly wounded in the First World War and never played again, while Wood, Gipps and Massey were mainly reserve team members during their time at White Hart Lane. The photograph also shows the houses in Paxton Road, which were demolished when the new east stand was put up in the 1930s.

In 1909, to mark Tottenham's election into the Football League, a new west stand was built. This view, taken in November of that year from the old south terrace (now known as the Park Lane stand), shows it in all its newly-built glory. Note the wooden crush barriers in the foreground. Mr Leitch, the architect, had designed other structures at the grounds of Fulham and Sunderland, and the new Spurs stand provided seating for 5,300 and an enclosure for another 6,000 spectators. It was officially opened for the first Tottenham home match versus Manchester United on 11 September 1909. A copper centrepiece consisting of a five-foot high cockerel was placed on the crest of the new stand in November. It was made by Braby the Coppersmiths of Euston Road, London, at a cost of £35. It has been moved around to different locations as the ground has been redeveloped and is now kept inside and undercover, while two replicas perch on the top of the west and east stands. The old west stand was re-roofed in 1934, and the ten supports seen in the picture were reduced to five.

Although Walter Tull spent only two years at Tottenham and made 18 appearances with 7 goals, he was one of the first black players to appear in the Football League. He had an English mother and a West Indian father, who died young leaving Walter to grow up in an orphanage. He shone at football while at school and came to Spurs via Clapton, leaving for Northampton in 1911. He attained the rank of sergeant in the First World War, but was killed in action in March 1918, just seven months before the Armistice.

Daniel Steele, the Tottenham captain, deciding the toss with the renowned Bob Crompton of Blackburn Rovers before the match at White Hart Lane on 28 March 1910. Spurs won the encounter 4-0, with Billy Minter scoring a hat-trick. Steele was a reserve with top Scottish club Rangers when Spurs signed him in 1906, where he again found himself an understudy, this time to Hughes and Morris – the two half-backs of the 1901 FA Cup-winning side. Establishing himself in 1908, he was an ever-present that season and was soon elected captain. He was released in 1912 and moved back to Scotland with Third Lanark.

Tottenham Hotspur *v.* Aston Villa on 19 November 1910, the Spurs' second season in the First Division. Unfortunately, Spurs went down 2-1 in this match, with centre forward Percy Humphreys scoring their goal. Lack of goals was the main reason that Spurs finished the season in fifteenth position, although they did manage a 6-2 victory over Middlesbrough (albeit in front of the lowest White Hart Lane crowd that season of 8,000). However, some silverware did find its way to Tottenham's shelf, the London Charity Cup being won by the reserve eleven with a 2-1 win over Fulham at Stamford Bridge. As can be seen, the Tottenham Palace was also in its heyday with top variety show stars performing there.

English League.   Kick-off 2.45 o'clock.

TOTTENHAM HOTSPUR.

RIGHT WING.   LEFT WING.

GOAL
LUNN
1

BACKS
ELKIN 2   BULLING 3

HALF-BACKS
BENTLEY 4   STEEL (D.) 5   DARNELL 6

FORWARDS
CURTIS 7   MINTER 8   HUMPHREYS 9   STEEL (R.) 10   MIDDLEMISS 11

Referee—Mr. T. GARNER.
Linesmen—Messrs. W. PERRY & A. H. MANNING.

EYRE 12   BACHE 13   HAMPTON 14   WALTERS 15   WALLACE 16
FORWARDS
HUNTER 17   BUCKLEY 18   TRANTER 19
HALF-BACKS
MILES 20   LYONS 21
BACKS
CARTLIDGE 22
GOAL
LEFT WING.   RIGHT WING.

ASTON VILLA.

ANY ALTERATIONS WILL BE NOTIFIED ON THE BOARD.

Charlie Rance started his playing career with Clapton when only fifteen years old and won an Amateur Cup winners' medal with them in 1907. He joined Tottenham in 1910 and held the centre half position – even through the First World War he made the most appearances for Spurs. He was an anchor for the 1919/20 Second Division championship team, but moved from Spurs in 1921. After spells with Derby and Queens Park Rangers he became manager at Guildford and coach with Wood Green.

Action from Tottenham Hotspur *v.* West Bromwich Albion, September 1911. The West Bromwich goalkeeper clears the ball from a group of Spurs forwards, including Billy Minter, who notched the only goal of the game for a 1-0 victory.

A late change of players somewhat disorganised the Spurs in this goalless draw at home to Sunderland in January 1912, and they had their goalkeeper Tom Lunn to thank for a brilliant performance. He is seen here punching away a shot. The other Spurs players are, from left to right: Webster, Lightfoot, Darnell, Steele, Collins, Curtis and Minter. Lunn had been a member of Wolves' FA Cup-winning team of 1908 and joined Tottenham in 1910. He was the regular custodian for two years, until he became a publican early in 1913. However, he incurred the wrath of the club's directors, as a result of which he was moved on.

A well-behaved section of the 17,000 crowd at the Spurs *v.* Sunderland match in January 1912. Items of interest are the lack of females amongst the spectators, the fact that everyone is wearing some headgear – mostly flat caps and bowlers – and a serviceman. They all seem quite pleased, although they saw no goals in this game. An end-of-season tour took Spurs into Europe again – they had been there the year before – playing eight games in four different countries in just twenty-two days, including one against Arsenal in Vienna.

Tottenham's first win in 1912 came at home to Middlesbrough by 2-1, Minter (in the first five minutes) and R. Steele being on target for Spurs. Billy Minter was the top scorer in this season with 21 goals. Newcomer Tom Mason made his debut in this game, but only appeared eight times before moving on. Tom Collins, the Spurs captain, is seen here spinning the coin at the start.

Tottenham players relaxing in 1912 with the footballer's typical extra pastime of golf. Taking a swing is Bert Middlemiss and he is accompanied by, from left to right: Ernie Newman, Tom Morris, Edward Lightfoot and Tom Collins. At this time the club's directors had taken over team selection and the signing of players after manager Fred Kirkham had resigned, but after four years of this arrangement a full-time manager was appointed again. In December 1912 Peter McWilliam took over the reigns and stayed for fourteen years.

Jabez Darnell, another Tottenham stalwart who served the club for many years, joined Spurs from Northampton in 1905. He remained a player for over fourteen years, but amazingly made only 327 appearances, scoring 5 goals from his wing half position. However, he was always on hand and never let the side down, missing only one game in Spurs' first season as a Football League club. He retired in 1919 and became assistant trainer, before going on to hold other backroom positions until 1946. Darnell passed away in 1950.

The Tottenham side of 1913/14. This team narrowly avoided relegation to the Second Division, ending the season three places from the bottom after a start of three consecutive victories. They finished the campaign with three defeats and no goals scored against ten conceded. Three of the 1921 FA Cup side were already at the club and are in this line-up. From left to right, back row: Webster, Weir, Steele, King, Grimsdell, Nie (trainer), Cartright. Front row: Walden, Fleming, Cantrell, Bliss, Oliver. One signing in January was that of Tommy Clay, who went straight into the team for the start of a long and illustrious career. Grimsdell, who had started his Tottenham career at centre half, missed only one match during 1913/14. At the end of the season, ignoring the possibility that the two countries would soon be at war, Spurs visited Germany. They were treated exceptionally well, apart from one town where any foreign side were treated to abuse, especially if they beat the home side. Spurs were unbeaten on this tour, which also took in Switzerland and Italy. It was reported that Tottenham signed a Berlin player, but at the declaration of war he had to quickly return to Germany and was never seen in the Tottenham colours.

'Titanic' Relief Fund.

("DAILY TELEGRAPH")

Football at Stadium

GREAT WHITE CITY, W.

WOOLWICH ARSENAL
V.
TOTTENHAM HOTSPUR

(Both Teams having volunteered their services)

ON

MONDAY, 29th APRIL

Gates open at 5 o'clock, and

KICK OFF AT SIX.

The free use of the Ground having been given by the Shepherd's Bush Exhibition Authorities, the

Entire Proceeds go to the Fund.

ADMISSION **6**d. and Upwards,   Boys Half-Price.

An interesting match was played at the White City in London on 29 April 1912, between Tottenham and Arsenal. This was in aid of the *Daily Telegraph's* relief fund for the Titanic, which had sunk a fortnight before with the loss of many lives. The handbill shows how the rivals pulled together on this occasion. For the record Arsenal won, but more important was the amount raised for the disaster fund.

Very little information is known about this photograph taken in 1915, only that they all worked at White Hart Lane and were recruited to form No. 1 Section 222 Field Co., Royal Engineers, under the command of Col Prescott and Lt E.J.L. Few MC. The Tottenham ground was used as a rifle range and drilling ground by the 4th Middlesex Regiment, and later commissioned by the War Office as a munitions factory. Spurs played their wartime matches at Highbury and Homerton. Thirteen players with Spurs connections lost their lives during the war.

Three

Between the Wars

The Tottenham Hotspur line-up in 1920. When soccer resumed after the First World War, Spurs were voted out of Division One and had to spend the next season in Division Two, which proved to be one of their best seasons ever. They started by winning their opening seven games, lost only four matches all season and remained unbeaten at home. They scored over 100 goals and took the championship six points clear of Huddersfield Town (in the days of two points for a win). From left to right, back row: R. McDonald, Forster, Goodman, Hunter, Jacques, French, Rance, Brown. Third row: Ross, Archibald, Smith, D. McDonald, Grimsdell, Walters, Pearson, Lowe, Skinner. Second row: Minter (trainer), O'Donnell, Castle, Clay, Wilson, Sage, Findlay, Lorimer, McWilliam (manager). Front row: Darnell (assistant trainer), Seed, Banks, Bliss, Dimmock, Chipperfield. Inset: Walden, Cantrell, Lindsay.

OUR PRINCE MEETS ARTHUR GRIMSDELL (OF THE "SPURS"

Many eminent visitors have paid a visit to White Hart Lane over the years. Here, Arthur Grimsdell, the Spurs captain, is shown meeting the Prince of Wales in 1920.

Two outstanding entertainers of the period shake hands: comedian Joe Elvin is on the left and the popular Fanny Walden on the right before a charity match featuring Spurs *v.* Music Hall artistes on 5 March 1923 at White Hart Lane.

On a training run around White Hart Lane on a damp November day in 1921 are, from left to right: Jimmy Skinner, Jimmy Seed and Tommy Clay. Skinner joined Spurs straight from his roots in Beckenham in Kent – mainly as an understudy for the England international wing halves at the club, Smith and Grimsdell – and only made 7 appearances during his first two seasons. He continued to serve the club well, playing in well over 100 matches until laid low by an injury. He then failed to comply with the training set out and was made available for transfer, but he decided to retire from the game.

The programme for Tottenham's second FA Cup success, beating Wolverhampton Wanderers by one Jimmy Dimmock goal to nil at Stamford Bridge in 1921. This was the second of three Cup Finals played at Chelsea's ground just after the First World War. At this time Spurs were in Division One and their opponents were from Division Two.

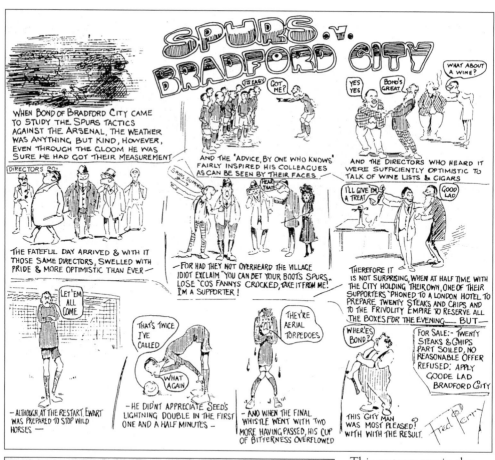

This cartoon was in the *Tottenham Herald* and shows how Spurs beat Bradford City in the FA Cup. Although Bradford came with high hopes, they found Spurs in fine form and a Seed hat-trick and a goal from Banks saw Tottenham through to the next round.

Jimmy Cantrell is just too late as Pearson, the West Bromwich Albion 'keeper, clears the ball in the Charity Shield match on Saturday 15 May 1920 at White Hart Lane.

A group of Tottenham supporters, dressed for the occasion, dance down the street in West London in April 1921. They are celebrating the club's second FA Cup final, twenty years after their first. The trophy was duly won, although five more League games were to be played – despite losing two of them Spurs finished in a respectable sixth place. To add to the silverware, they captured the Charity Shield by beating Burnley on 16 May 1921.

King George V meeting the Tottenham team before the 1921 Cup Final. The morning of 23 April was wet, but the conditions were ignored and nearly 73,000 packed into Stamford Bridge – the gates were closed at 2.20 p.m., forty minutes before the kick-off. The King and his son, the Duke of York, walked out in the heavy rain to greet the teams. The pitch soon resembled a lake, but both Spurs and Wolves put on a brave show under the conditions.

Jimmy Dimmock, a real Tottenham legend, signed as an amateur from Edmonton Ramblers in 1918 and stayed until 1931. He went straight from school onto Spurs' books, although he was allowed to assist Clapton Orient during the First World War. He only represented England 3 times, but this fails to record the true image of a very skilful player, and also a popular one as well. Altogether he made 491 appearances for Spurs and scored 138 goals, his FA Cup-winning strike ensuring him a place in Spurs' history. This most famous of his goals happened when Dimmock received the ball from his left-wing partner Bert Bliss and started off on one of his usual runs, which the clogging mud had foiled previously during the match. The supporters moaned at first but became excited as he made his way goalwards, until he was tackled and lost the ball. However, just as quickly Jimmy regained possession and sent in a low drive which eluded the clutching hands of the Wolves goalkeeper to rest snugly in the net. Dimmock ended his career with a season for Thames in 1931, before moving on to Orient and Ashford. He suffered a lot of ill health in his latter days and passed away in the North Middlesex Hospital in 1972.

Sweeping out of the gates at Stamford Bridge in 1921 are the Tottenham team with the FA Cup proudly displayed on the front of their charabanc. Captain Arthur Grimsdell was missing, however – he had modestly slipped away back home to Watford at the earliest convenient moment, leaving the celebrating to the other team members.

Arthur Grimsdell was a schoolboy star and a member of his local team at seventeen; Tottenham signed him a year later. He was to become a special member of the Spurs for the next eighteen years, leading the team as captain for most of them. An England international, he excelled both in attack and defence. A measure of his influence was shown when he had a long spell off injured and the side struggled markedly without him. On leaving Spurs he had a year at Clapton Orient, before turning to coaching schoolboys, finally becoming a director of his hometown, Watford.

Tottenham Hotspur's FA Cup-winning team line-up in 1921. From left to right, back row: Minter (trainer), Clay, Smith, Hunter, Walters, McDonald. Front row: Banks, Seed, Grimsdell, Cantrell, Bliss, Dimmock. Two disappointed players were Fanny Walden and Bill Jaques, who were regulars in the side until injury lost them their place and an FA Cup winners' medal. On their way to the final, Spurs had beaten Bristol Rovers, Bradford City, Southend United, Aston Villa and Preston North End. When the team reached Tottenham with the trophy, police struggled to clear a path for the procession, which was led by the Tottenham Town Band. The cup itself was adorned with the same blue and white ribbons that had been tied onto it in 1901, the last time Spurs had won it. A celebration dinner held at the Holborn Restaurant was chaired by Charles Roberts and included as a guest Commander Ralph Bullock CBE, one of the club's original directors, and also ten of the 1901 side (Clawley had died). Each member of the 1921 team received a gold watch from the club, who also recognized the service of the trainer Billy Minter by presenting him with a watch as well.

The England eleven who faced Scotland in Glasgow on 9 April 1921 included four Tottenham players, the most seen together in the England shirt. Unfortunately, Scotland went on to win 3-0. From left to right, back row: Bert Smith (Spurs), Harry Chambers (Liverpool), Tom Smart (Aston Villa), Harold Gough (Sheffield United), Jack Silcock (Manchester United), George Wilson (Sheffield Wednesday). Front row: Sam Chedgzoy (Everton), Bob Kelly (Burnley), Arthur Grimsdell (Spurs), Bert Bliss (Spurs), Jimmy Dimmock (Spurs). Of the 1921 Spurs side that won the cup, Tommy Clay had already been capped for England and Jimmy Seed was in the side against Belgium in May 1921.

It was in January 1914 that Tommy Clay joined Tottenham from Leicester Fosse. He was born in Leicester and, after two seasons with his local side, he so impressed Spurs manager Peter McWilliam that he was quickly signed. He was capped for England in the early 1920s and once played in goal for Spurs at Sunderland, when the two specialist goalkeepers were injured. In 1929 he took on the player-coach position at Spurs' nursery club Northfleet, and later kept a public house at St Albans. He passed away in 1949.

53

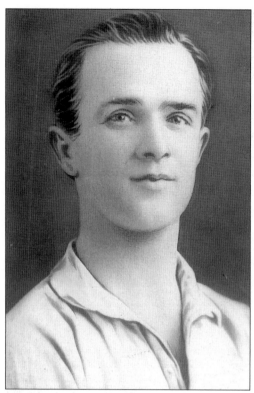

Fred Walden, known to any true Spurs supporter as 'Fanny', paraded his talents on the Tottenham right wing for fourteen seasons from 1912 to 1926, playing twice for England in 1914 and 1922. A diminutive man, standing at just over five feet, he cost Spurs £1,700 when he transferred from Northampton Town. He was also a cricketer of note with Northamptonshire throughout his football career, scoring over 7,000 runs and taking over 100 wickets in 258 county matches. He became an umpire after retiring and reached Test match level.

The main gate and entrance to White Hart Lane in 1922. The photograph shows the old Red House on the right, while the car is parked outside the White Hart public house on the left. This view remained relatively unaltered from 1910 until the west stand was developed in the 1980s.

Peter McWilliam had two spells as manager of Tottenham Hotspur, initially from 1912 to 1927 and then returning in May 1938. He was one of the first men to win the FA Cup both as a player (with Newcastle United in 1911) and as a manager (with Spurs in 1921). Born in Inverness, McWilliam won three League Championships with Newcastle and was a Scottish international. Joining Tottenham a second time, he soon began to promote youngsters from the nursery club at Northfleet, seeing the future as being in their hands, but the war halted his plans and he retired in 1942.

"There has been too much rough play in first-class football this season. No, I do not blame the bonus system. Some, I know, think that the fact of players receiving two pounds for a win stimulates undue keenness and unscrupulous tactics. But that is not my view. It is my opinion that the real culprit is that much-maligned person, the referee. Too much leniency has been displayed by these all-important officials."—Tom Clay (the Spurs' back).

Nothing is ever new in football circles, as is indicated by this cutting from the *All Sports* magazine in January 1922, which quotes Spurs' well-known right-back, Tommy Clay, and his view on foul tactics.

Action from Tottenham v. Chelsea, in front of a crowd of 54,000 at Stamford Bridge, on 24 January 1922. Bert Bliss is shown scoring the first of his two goals, which beat the home side 2-0. This season saw Spurs finish in second spot in Division One, also reaching the semi-finals of the FA Cup, where they went down narrowly to Preston North End 2-1.

Arsenal v. Tottenham at Highbury on 30 September 1922. Spurs goalkeeper Herbert Blake is beaten by White of Arsenal but the 'goal' was ruled offside. Two legitimate strikes from Dimmock gave Spurs a sweet victory as only the week before an ill-tempered game at White Hart Lane had resulted in Bert Smith being ordered off in a 2-1 Spurs win.

It's Saturday and here come the Spurs for their first match of the 1923/24 season, at home to Preston North End. Following Tommy Clay are the two Jimmy's – Dimmock and Seed. Although getting away to a good start with four wins and a draw in the first six matches, Tottenham failed to settle into any rhythm over this season, even going out of the FA Cup at the first hurdle to Crystal Palace (a Division Two side at the time) 2-0.

Being so close, Tottenham and Clapton Orient had many players who moved between the two clubs, mainly from Spurs to Orient. Included in a large list are Danny Steel, Archibald and several members of the cup side of 1921: Grimsdell, Seed, Bliss, Dimmock and McDonald. Later, Billy Rees and Ken Flint made the switch. The Orient team pictured here shows Bert Bliss (sitting one in from the far right of the photograph).

Charlie Handley was a stalwart in the Tottenham side from 1921 to 1929 – although never quite a regular, he filled several different positions. At five feet seven inches, he was a player who never stood out, and of course he was soon nicknamed 'Tich'. He was another local lad from Edmonton made good. After leaving Spurs he could not settle at any other club and went to Switzerland to help old Spur Bert Smith in coaching for a while before retiring.

The programme for Spurs v. Sunderland on 24 January 1925. This match was also a testimonial for Bob Brown, Bert Smith and Jimmy Skinner. There were no special games arranged for testimonials at this time, the beneficiaries receiving the proceeds from a League match such as this one.

Tottenham Hotspur FC line-up, 1923/24. From left to right, back row: Skinner, Brown, Walters, Bunn, Purdey, Maddison, Blake, McDonald, Clay, Duffus, Ross, Ives. Third row: W. Over (groundsman), W. Minter, Banks, White, Forster, B. Smith, Grimsdell, Lowe, Skitt, Bann, Sage, Thompson. Second row: C.D. Roberts, M. Cadman, T. Deacock, Elkes, McCudden, Dimmock, Seed, Sharp, Jennings, G. Cox, F. Bearman, P. McWilliam (manager). Front row: Barnett, Handley, Walden, W. Smith, Lindsay, Brooks. The highest goalscorer this season was Alec Lindsay with 21. Lindsay had spent several years as understudy for Jimmy Cantrell, who played his last game for Spurs at the age of forty. Lindsay lost his place to Osborne a few years later, but continued to play anywhere and held down a team spot until moving back to Scotland (Dundee) in 1930. Surprisingly, Fanny Walden played his last game during this season, although he remained on the club's books for two more years. It was also the last season for goalkeeper Herbert Blake, who had been twenty-seven when he joined Spurs and after 62 appearances was given a free transfer, moving to Kettering Town in 1925. The Park Lane end of the ground was covered during this season at a cost of £3,000 and three sides of White Hart Lane were now under cover.

Action from the Cardiff City *v.* Tottenham Hotspur FA Cup-tie at Ninian Park on 24 February 1923. Herbert Blake is clearing from the Cardiff forwards, helped by Smith and watched by Grimsdell, who played at right-back in this game. The Spurs player with his back to camera is Brown. Spurs won the match 3-2, although this was the year that they nearly went out the cup to Worksop Town, drawing 0-0 at White Hart Lane before making sure of progression in the replay by winning 9-0.

Tottenham players and the Notts County team stand in tribute to the late Queen Alexandra at Meadow Lane in November 1925. Amongst the Spurs team (in their change strip of hooped shirts) are Clay and Dimmock (on the extreme left), Seed (on the right), goalkeeper Kane, Elkes, Osborne, Skinner and Smith.

Tottenham Hotspur FC, 1924/25. From left to right, back row: Jack Elkes, Cecil Poynton, Tommy Clay, Fred Hinton, Harry Hargreaves, Buchanan Sharp, Harry Lowe. Front row: Frank Osborne, Bert Smith, Jimmy Seed, Alec Lindsay, Arthur Grimsdell, Jimmy Skinner, Jimmy Dimmock. This was a mediocre season for Spurs, ending in a mid-table position. Goals were hard to come by and inside forward Jimmy Seed ended up top marksman with 20 goals (having hit the target only twice in the season before and following it up with just six the next campaign). Three centre forwards were tried but could only muster eighteen goals between them. New goalkeeper Hinton had been signed from Bolton Wanderers the year before, and was an ever-present in the team, saving possibly his best performance for the two FA Cup matches against his former club, which drew 50,000 to each game. Spurs won through 1-0 at Bolton after a 1-1 result at White Hart Lane, which the local press described as 'one of the finest cup struggles ever staged on the High Road enclosure'. Apart from the cup games, which acted as a magnet for the crowds, 54,000 was the highest attendance for the home match against Blackburn Rovers. The crowd figures often reflected the mediocre displays: 8,000 for the game against Leeds being the lowest, whilst even cup holders Newcastle and rivals Arsenal could only attract just over 20,000 to White Hart Lane. Spanish club Real Madrid toured Britain during the season and, on a Thursday afternoon in March, took on Spurs Reserves, who won 4-2. This game was attended by the Spanish Ambassador, who was reported to have been 'occupying the royal box'.

SPORTPLATZ LANDHOF

Preis 20 Cts.

Phot. Jeck · Das hervorragende englische Team der Tottenham Hotspurs, (Cliché »Schweizer Sport«) welches zur Zeit in der Schweiz gastiert und überall bewunderungswürdigen Sport zeigt. Von links nach rechts : Hinton, Schindelwiller, Wilfe, Hartley, Dimmock, Grimsdell, Lane, Skitt, Smith, Seed, Clay, Hinton, Thompson.

Sonntag, 24. Mai 1925, nachmittags 3ʰ

TOTTENHAM HOTSPURS

gegen **F. C. BASEL** verstärkt

1 Uhr

Vorspiel

SCHUHHAUS

JAKOB **KALLER**

BARFÜSSERPLATZ 18

Spurs' first foreign tour following the First World War was to Switzerland, where they played 7 matches and won them all, scoring 29 goals and conceding just 2. This programme, one of the best produced by such a small country, was for the last match of the tour and pictures the Tottenham side that opposed FC Basel.

Jack Elkes arrived at Tottenham for £1,000 in 1923, via Birmingham and Southampton. Standing at six feet tall, he was a useful inside forward and scored 57 goals in his 213 appearances for Spurs. He was unlucky not to play for England, being a member of the FA party that toured Australia in 1925. At times his height made him a more-than-capable stand-in centre half. Not retained in 1929, he played non-League football until retiring in 1937.

Arsenal *v.* Tottenham, 1925. This was the first match of the season and Arsenal unveiled their new signing, Charles Buchan, but Spurs were the victors with a Jimmy Dimmock goal. The action shows Buchan winning a heading duel with Tommy Clay. The other Spurs players are Harry Skitt (back to camera), Jimmy Seed (half hidden) and Jimmy Skinner (watching on the right).

Action from the 1926 meeting between Spurs and Everton, again the first match of a new season, which Spurs won 2-1. Jim Smith, the Spurs goalkeeper, is punching the ball clear. The other white shirts are: Elkes (jumping with his 'keeper) and Matt Forster (on the right). James McQueen Anderson Smith was at the club when the goalkeeping spot was a problem and he contested the jersey with five other goalies during his two-year stay. He went back to Scotland after 36 matches and later appeared for Norwich City for one season.

Gallaher's Cigarettes.

Gallaher's Cigarettes.

A 1-1 draw was the result of this 1925 FA Cup-tie versus Bolton Wanderers at White Hart Lane. The opposing player in the striped shirt is J.R. Smith of Bolton, whilst the two Spurs players are Grimsdell (on the left) and McDonald. Lane got Tottenham's winner in the replay.

The Tottenham programme, although said to be quite sparse, always carried a cartoon-type cover early on. This one, for the fixture with Newcastle, the League Champions at the time, on 7 January 1928, featured 'Cocky' – a Fred Perry creation who appeared until the late 1920s. Here, our hero bemoans the fact that Spurs have been frozen out of League points over the Christmas period.

This is a newspaper report of Tottenham's first game back in Division Two on 25 August 1928, having being relegated after finishing one place off the bottom the previous season. The club were worried that, being in the Second Division once more, the spectators would desert them, but over 33,000 turned up for this first match and saw Spurs win 4-1 against Oldham. Frank Osborne, Jack Elkes and newcomer Tom Roberts (with two goals), were the marksmen. The goals from Roberts were his only goals for Tottenham as injuries limited his outings to just four games.

A new artist took over the front of the programme from 1928 onwards. Jos Walker's forte was sketches of the players and 'Cocky' disappeared from the scene. This programme cover depicts ace marksman Ted Harper, who had scored seven goals in the first two games of the season.

The 1927/28 season was not a good one for Tottenham, for as well as suffering relegation they went out of the FA Cup with a 6-1 defeat at Huddersfield. Eugene 'Taffy' O'Callaghan is shown here scoring Spurs' only goal of the match.

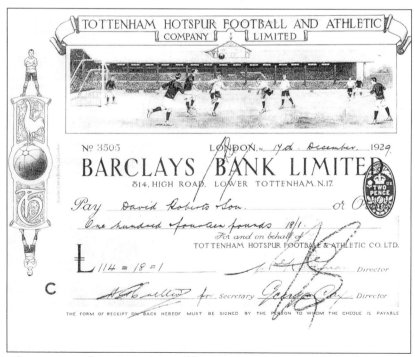

A Tottenham vignette from 1929; cheques like this are not seen anymore. This specimen shows a fine view of the old west stand.

At the end of the 1928/29 season, Tottenham made a tour of Malta – this was the first time that they had visited the island. Here, they are seen facing the camera with their opponents before one of the matches, all of which attracted large crowds. Spurs won all of the six games they played, including two against the British Army and the Royal Navy, as well as Sliema, Valetta and Floriana. Tottenham remain one of the most popular teams amongst Maltese football supporters, and today have one of the overseas branches of the Spurs Supporters Club in their own café and club in Valetta

The programme cover for the visit of Chelsea on 1 February 1930 shows Spurs manager Percy Smith together with Chelsea heading for the glamour of Division One. Unfortunately, Tottenham fell by the wayside, but Chelsea managed to step up that season. The game ended in a 3-3 draw, Thompson, Harper and Cook netting for Spurs.

Cyril Spiers was Tottenham's goalkeeper for nearly five seasons. Originally from the Midlands, he started his professional career with Aston Villa where, having established himself in the side, he spent seven years. An injury left Aston Villa undecided about his recovery and they decided that he would not be able to play again. After he had undergone an operation in the close season, Spurs stepped in to offer him a trial for a month when regular Tottenham goalkeeper Jock Britton was sidelined after a motorcycle accident. Spiers' performances during the trial period earned him a permanent place in the Spurs goal for the next four years. He proved tough and reliable, and also good enough to play for the Football League XI against the Scottish League in 1930. Indeed, Spiers came close to selection for England when he played in the international trial match in March 1931, but found the current England 'keeper, Hibbs, too difficult to displace. He left Tottenham in May 1933 and went back to the Midlands to Wolves, before moving into management with Cardiff, Norwich, Crystal Palace and Exeter City.

The Tottenham Hotspur official club photograph for the 1930/31 season. From left to right, back row: Alsford, Thompson, Cable, Harper, Messer, Spiers, Nicholls, Taylor, Rowley, Herod, Lyons, Poynton, Osborne. Middle row: G. Hardy (trainer), Minter, Darnell, Evans, Rowe, Bellamy, Lowdell, Skitt, Hartley, Hodgkinson, Reddish, Dimmock, Howe, Gordon, W. Over (groundsman), J. Anderson, H. Crellin, B. Ives. Front row: A. Turner (secretary), G. Wagstaff-Simmons, C.D. Roberts (chairman), Channell, O'Callaghan, Scott, Hunt, Cook, Ison, Illingworth, Smy, Meads, M. Cadman, G. Cox, P. Smith (manager). Insets: Davies, F.J. Bearman. New signings in this season included George Hunt (from Chesterfield), Alf Messer (Reading) and Albert Lyons (Clapton Orient). Spurs played in front of royalty when they were the opposition at West Ham in a charity match for the British Legion funds, attended by HRH the Prince of Wales, later King Edward VIII. This become yet another nearly season that saw Spurs, lying in second place in February, falter rather badly, winning only four of their last fourteen League matches. As a result, they ended up in third position and missed out on promotion. The season had started with a bang in the shape of a 7-1 victory over Reading (Ted Harper notching five of the goals), and an 8-1 thrashing of Burnley. Thus it was a very confident Spurs side that went to their third match at Wolverhampton Wanderers, but alas they bit the dust and lost 3-1. Their only excuse was that they lost left-back Bert Hodgkinson with a dislocated shoulder, and being two down found themselves unable to pull the game around.

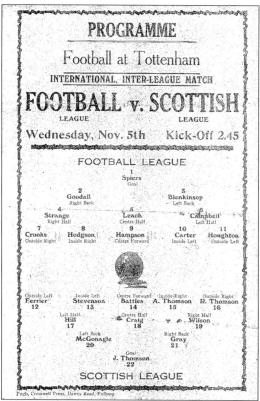

PROGRAMME

Football at Tottenham

INTERNATIONAL, INTER-LEAGUE MATCH

FOOTBALL v. SCOTTISH
LEAGUE   LEAGUE

Wednesday, Nov. 5th   Kick-Off 2.45

FOOTBALL LEAGUE

1
Spiers
Goal

2
Goodall
Right Back

3
Blenkinsop
Left Back

4
Strange
Right Half

5
Leach
Centre Half

6
Campbell
Left Half

7
Crooks
Outside Right

8
Hodgson
Inside Right

9
Hampson
Centre Forward

10
Carter
Inside Left

11
Houghton
Outside Left

Outside Left
Ferrier
12

Inside Left
Stevenson
13

Centre Forward
Battles
14

Inside Right
A. Thomson
15

Outside Right
R. Thomson
16

Left Half
Hill
17

Centre Half
Craig
18

Right Half
Wilson
19

Left Back
McGonagle
20

Right Back
Gray
21

Goal
J. Thomson
22

SCOTTISH LEAGUE

Pugh, Cromwell Press, Dawes Road, Fulham

Pirate programmes are nothing new. This one was on sale outside White Hart Lane for the meeting of the Football League and the Scottish League on 5 November 1930. Clubs soon noticed the fact that these unofficial programmes existed and frequently recommended to their supporters that they should be avoided. It was mainly the successful clubs who attracted private programme sellers, who normally targetted visiting supporters who did not know what the home team's official programme looked like. These artefacts have now become collectors' items in their own right.

Pictured in 1931, Percy Smith the Tottenham manager talks tactics with, from left to right: Dimmock, Messer, Davies, Cook, Harper, Lyons, Hodgkinson and Rowe. It was Smith who brought George Hunt to Tottenham and he quickly made his mark with 25 goals for the reserve team in his first season.

A letter from manager Percy Smith, dated 10 February 1931, informing a new player of his selection for a match. Note that the teams travelled to their games by charabanc.

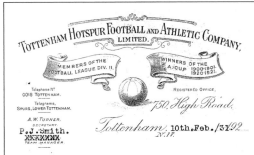

TOTTENHAM HOTSPUR FOOTBALL AND ATHLETIC COMPANY, LIMITED.

MEMBERS OF THE FOOTBALL LEAGUE DIV. II.

WINNERS OF THE F.A.CUP 1900-1901. 1920-1921.

Telephone No. 0018 TOTTENHAM.
Telegrams, SPURS, LOWER TOTTENHAM.
A.W. TURNER. SECRETARY.
P.J. Smith. TEAM MANAGER.

REGISTERED OFFICE,
750. High Road.
Tottenham, 10th. Feb./31 192
N. 17.

Dear Mr. Briggs,

I should be pleased if you can assist us, on Saturday next 14th. Feb. against Northfleet, at Northfleet.

We leave our ground here at 12.30pm. and travel to Northfleet by charabanc, please let me know by return if you can play, & if so, will you be on our ground here at 12.30pm.

Kind regards,

Yours faithfully,
P.J. Smith
Team Manager.

W.J. Briggs, Esq.,
Selby Cottage,
The Terrace, Fishergate.

Wally Alsford, a local Edmonton lad, came up through the junior ranks and made his first senior appearance in 1930 against Reading. Never a real regular, one of his best seasons was 1934/35 and, although Tottenham were relegated at the end of it, Wally played his one and only match for England against Scotland at Hampden Park. Transferring to Nottingham Forest in January 1937, he was forced to retire after only one season because of illness.

Tottenham's White Hart Lane pitch had caused some concern over the years and these two pictures show attempts to rectify the matter in the 1930s. The top image shows the laying of more drainage pipes along the edge of the pitch near the west stand and the bottom one shows the laying of new turf over the whole ground.

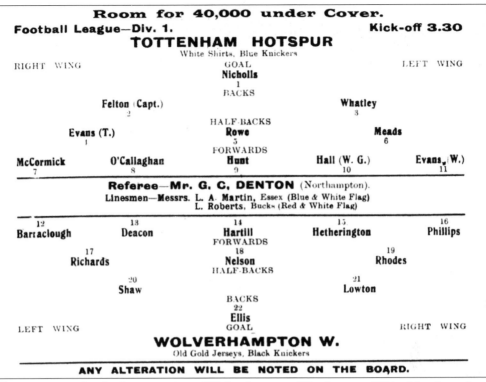

Room for 40,000 under Cover.

Football League—Div. 1.   Kick-off 3.30

TOTTENHAM HOTSPUR
White Shirts, Blue Knickers

RIGHT WING   GOAL   LEFT WING

Nicholls
1
BACKS

Felton (Capt.)   **Whatley**
2   3

HALF-BACKS

Evans (T.)   **Rowe**   **Meads**
1   5   6

FORWARDS

McCormick   **O'Callaghan**   **Hunt**   **Hall (W. G.)**   **Evans (W.)**
7   8   9   10   11

Referee—Mr. G. C. DENTON (Northampton).
Linesmen—Messrs. L. A. Martin, Essex (Blue & White Flag)
L. Roberts, Bucks (Red & White Flag)

12   13   14   15   16
Barraclough   **Deacon**   **Hartill**   **Hetherington**   **Phillips**
FORWARDS

17   18   19
Richards   **Nelson**   **Rhodes**
HALF-BACKS

20   21
Shaw   **Lowton**

BACKS
22
Ellis
LEFT WING   GOAL   RIGHT WING

WOLVERHAMPTON W.
Old Gold Jerseys, Black Knickers

ANY ALTERATION WILL BE NOTED ON THE BOARD.

The programme for the first ever visit of Wolverhampton Wanderers to White Hart Lane for a Division One match on Monday 28 August 1933. Spurs won 4-0 with two goals each from Taffy O'Callaghan and George Hunt. The visitors had been building a team to get them into the top flight and, like the Spurs, it had done the trick.

Tottenham's defence at work in the 1932 Division Two home match against Oldham Athletic, with Arthur Rowe getting one in the eye in the 1-1 draw. Also in the photograph are Felton (back to the camera) and Whatley (crouching on the left).

Percy Smith, the former Bury manager, guided Tottenham back to the First Division. He took over from Billy Minter, who had been in charge for two years. Smith had been a player with Preston and Blackburn Rovers, and was responsible for the inspirational signings of George Hunt, Willie Evans and Willie Hall during his spell in charge of Tottenham.

Members of the Tottenham Hotspur party leaving Euston Station for an FA Cup-tie at Oldham in 1933. George Hunt is holding a magazine with O'Callaghan and trainer George Hardy on his left. Wally Alsford and Dave Colquhoun are behind them. The players returned with smiles after a 6-0 victory, with Hunt getting a hat-trick. However, they failed to clear the next hurdle, losing at Luton Town.

Action from Spurs *v*. Aston Villa in September 1933. The Tottenham players are, from left to right, Rowe, Tom Evans, Bill Felton and O'Callaghan. Their target is Villa's Waring, who is attacking the Paxton Road end. Goals from O'Callaghan, Hunt and a penalty from Willie Evans gave the home side a 3-2 victory.

Fred Channell was another local lad who progressed through the Tottenham nursery clubs from school. He made his first League appearance for Spurs against Sunderland in 1933 and quickly settled in the side. He was looked upon as a future England player, but a serious injury forced his retirement at the age of twenty-six. For a while he ran a sports shop practically opposite White Hart Lane in the High Road.

E. HARPER. Centre Forward.
Height 5ft. 10½in., weight 11st. 7lb.
Born at Sheppey Island. Played for
Blackburn Rovers and Sheffield Wednes-
day. International v. Scotland, 1926.

Ted Harper, born at Sheerness in Kent, was the Tottenham centre forward from 1928 to 1932, and a prolific scorer who could have got many more, but for the hard handling that he came in for when his reputation became known. He was signed from Sheffield Wednesday and his 78 Tottenham appearances brought him 83 goals – a record that is hard to better. Strangely, he was only capped once by England, against Scotland in 1926. Harper set a (then) Spurs record by scoring 36 goals in a single season (1930/31).

One of the best forward lines ever paraded by Tottenham was in the 1933/34 season. From left to right: Willie Evans (21 goals), Willie Hall (4 goals and playing in all the games), George Hunt (37 goals), Jimmy McCormick (9 goals) and Taffy O'Callaghan (13 goals). A highlight of the season was the 3-1 victory over Arsenal at Highbury – the Gunners' first home defeat of that season.

LNER Locomotive B17 No. 2830 was named 'Tottenham Hotspur'. Originally called 'Thoresby Park' in 1931, it was renamed after the club in January 1938, when locomotive 2870, the original Spurs railway engine, was streamlined and its name changed. The locomotive, seen passing Alexandra Palace, was withdrawn from service in 1958.

Tottenham Hotspur FC, 1933/34. From left to right, back row: George Hardy (trainer), Tom Meads, Almer Hall, Bill Felton, Joe Nicholls, Wally Alsford, George Greenfield, Les Howe, Percy Smith (manager). Middle row: Fred Channell, Bill Whatley, Tom Evans, Arthur Rowe, Jimmy McCormick, Dave Colquhoun. Front row: Taffy O'Callaghan, George Hunt, Willie Hall, Willie Evans. This was one of the better years for Spurs in the top division, finishing in third spot and pulling in some big crowds, the highest at White Hart Lane being 56,612 for the visit of Arsenal.

Tottenham Hotspur FC, 1934/35. From left to right, back row: Goldsmith, Sargent, D. Hunt, Ivory, Alsford, Nicholls, Taylor, Jones, Buckingham, Meads, Hall, Colquhoun. Third row: G. Hardy (trainer), Brain, King, Levene, Rowe, Channell, Whatley, Day, Phypers, Illingworth, Greenfield, Morrison, J. Anderson, W. Over. Second row: J. Darnell, Ives, P. Smith (manager), F. Bearman, M. Cadman, C.D. Roberts (chairman), G. Cox, G.W. Simmons, A. Turner (secretary), W. Minter. Front row: O'Callaghan, Bellamy, McCormick, T. Evans, G. Hunt, Howe, Bolan, Hedley, Potts, W. Evans. Third position the previous season gave great hope for success during this campaign, but relegation followed as injuries to key players hit the team hard, and they won only 2 of their last 20 League games. The top scorer was Willie Evans, with only 12 goals, which tells a story in itself. George Greenfield, a promising player who had broken his leg the year before, retired after attempting a comeback. The FA Cup gave a small ray of hope when Spurs beat Manchester City and Newcastle before going out to Bolton – over 70,000 were at White Hart Lane for the first Bolton match. The popular Taffy O'Callaghan moved to Leicester in mid-season. However, the reserve side gave aspirations for a brighter future by finishing second in the Combination, with a total of 124 goals in 46 matches. Thirty-six different players were used in the first team during the season, the most since the First World War. Four new players were signed and Fred Sargent was brought into the team from the junior squad, but it was all to no avail as the team plunged to the foot of the table. Manager Percy Smith handed in his resignation before the end of the season, leaving Walter Hardinge in charge.

Tottenham made regular tours to the Channel Islands between the wars and they are pictured here with their hosts on the 1935 trip. They played two matches, winning both by 5-0, the first against Guernsey and the second against a Channel Island XI on Guernsey, which was when this photograph was taken on 16 May. Tottenham chairman Mr C.D. Roberts is sitting bareheaded in the centre of the front row and trainer George Hardy is first left on the second row. Other Spurs players (in white shirts) are, from left to right, middle row: Almer Hall, Charles Jones, Wally Alsford, Joe Nicholls, Fred Channell, Willie Hall. Front row: Foster Hedley, Len Bolan, Doug Hunt, Les Howe, Jim Fullwood. It is interesting to note that some Spurs players were taken along to the Castel School while on the island, to pass on some coaching tips to a class of boys. Amongst those schoolboys was ten-year-old Len Duquemin, later to become one of the island's most famous football heroes when he joined Spurs after the Second World War.

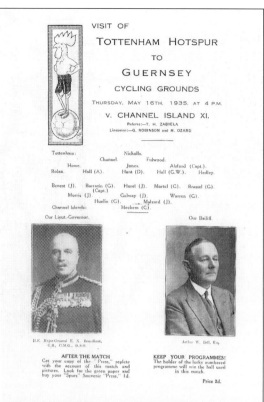

The programme for the Tottenham *v.* Channel Island XI match on 16 May 1935. The game was played at the 'Cycling Ground' on Guernsey. On the Spurs right wing was Len Bolan, in one of his 13 games for the club, and at centre half Charlie Jones, appearing in one of only 19 matches for Spurs.

A scene not seen so much in modern day football: Spurs' own laundress is working overtime on washing day in 1935 and is being helped by a member of the ground staff with the pegging out of twenty-two shirts, shorts and pairs of socks.

Architect Archibald Leitch was again given the job of designing and overseeing the building of a new stand at White Hart Lane with the ambitious new double-decker East Stand. This was erected in 1934, opening for the visit of Aston Villa on 22 September. Shown here during its construction, it provided seating for 4,983 with another 109 special seats in the 'crow's-nest' feature towering above the new stand. A boys' enclosure, with a capacity of just over 1,000, became a feature in the south-east corner of the ground, while a favourite spot for many fans on the bottom terrace was the 'shelf'.

The new stand meant that the private houses along the east side of the stadium had to be demolished and the residents rehoused at a cost to the club of around £5,000 – the whole project costing almost £60,000. This photograph shows a room of one of those houses being pulled down. A fireplace can be seen on the left

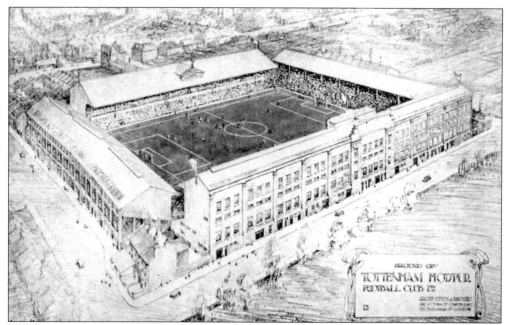

A drawing by the architect showing how White Hart Lane looked from the air after the changes in 1934. Note the small houses still occupying a corner space in the foreground. The new east stand put the capacity of the stadium at 80,000 and the club boasted that 60,000 could be accommodated under cover.

England Test cricketer Bill Edrich was also a fine footballer, and after playing at Norwich as an amateur, Tottenham signed him as a professional. He played at outside left for Spurs between 1935 and 1937. Cricket was his first love, however, and reluctantly Spurs released him to tour with the England cricket team. Edrich played a handful of games for Chelmsford when he was in the RAF.

Tottenham Hotspur FC, 1935/36. With a new manager, Jack Tresadern, the Spurs finished fifth in the Second Division as they tried to bounce straight back to the top flight. From left to right, back row: Howe, Channell, Taylor, Hunt, Whatley, Phypers. Front row: Sargent, Almerhall, Morrison, W. Hall, Evans, Rowe. In mid-December they were top of the table, but two unexpected defeats by Plymouth over Christmas left them with too much leeway to make up. Ralph Ward and Joe Meek were signed from Bradford Park Avenue during the campaign to boost the attempt to regain lost ground, and teenager Albert Hall made his debut. The goals tally was high this year with 91 scored in the League and 101 in all games. The pre-season practice match ended 4-4 in front of 9,000, while the reserve eleven chalked up a 12-1 win over Crystal Palace in their first match – Morrison, Almerhall and Sargent all getting three goals. The first team also showed they could score with a 7-2 win against Swansea and an 8-0 against Southampton. Spurs also reached the last eight in the FA Cup. They were paired with Southend United in the first round, whom they beat in a replay after drawing at White Hart Lane. Huddersfield and Bradford were then dispatched before Sheffield United put an end to the Tottenham cup dream for another season. During this season a crowd of 54,186 fans were attracted to White Hart Lane to watch England defeat Germany 3-0 on a Wednesday afternoon in December.

Tottenham *v.* Arsenal in 1935, when the old rivals inflicted a home defeat on Spurs. This photograph shows George Hunt's header being collected by Arsenal's goalkeeper, Frank Moss, with Spurs winger McCormick in the background.

Captain Willie Hall extends a welcome to Andy Duncan, who arrived at Tottenham from Hull City in March 1935 for a transfer fee of £6,000. Duncan played quite regularly for four years and managed to turn out frequently during the war. He played his final game for Spurs in bizarre circumstances against Crystal Palace on 29 August 1942, when he walked off the pitch after suffering some barracking, saying 'I'm finished'. True to his word, he never played for the club again.

CARTOON BY TOM WEBSTER

HISTORIC CUP TIE : 1937—Tottenham 4, Everton 3

(Reprinted by permission of the 'Daily Mail')

The Daily Mail carried this cartoon by the notable Tom Webster, reflecting the exciting FA Cup-tie between Tottenham and Everton in 1937, also covering the replay – which provided a rousing ending. With under half an hour left to play, Spurs were 3-1 in arrears. They then came to life to spectacularly draw level, before in the last seconds Jack Morrison grabbed the Spurs' winner, completing his own hat-trick in the process.

Prior to an FA Cup match at White Hart Lane on 25 January 1936, Tottenham Hotspur and Huddersfield Town stand for a moment in silence to mark the death of King George V. Spurs

went on to win the fourth round tie with a Les Howe goal before their biggest gate of the season, 64,149.

Action from the FA Cup replay, between Tottenham and Everton, at White Hart Lane on 22 February 1937, showing Everton's Sagar saving from Morrison. In the 1-1 draw at Goodison, Jack Hall had saved a penalty from Everton's formidable Dixie Dean to set up the replay.

Photographs of reserve teams are not seen very often. This one features the Tottenham Reserves of 1937/38. From left to right, back row: Ludford, Dann, Spelman, Hooper, Martin, Reeves, Jeffrey. Front row: McCormick, Meek, G. Hunt, A. Hall, Wilkins, Hitchins. George Ludford had forced his way to the forefront with a record total of 101 goals for Spurs' nursery side, Northfleet, in 1935/36.

Yorkshire-born George Hunt joined Spurs from Chesterfield in 1930 and made rapid progress, playing 3 times for England. He was arguably the best signing made by manager Percy Smith, who jumped in when others dallied. He was rewarded when Hunt began to score with astonishing regularity and led the team to promotion in 1933. When he left Tottenham in 1937, he had netted 151 goals in 205 appearances.

The programme for the visit of Coventry City on 3 September 1938. The cartoon on the cover of this issue features captain Willie Hall, who apparently had lost the toss for ends at the last few matches.

Spurs provided several players for representative matches during the 1930s. This is a photograph of the Football League team who opposed the Scottish League in 1938. From left to right, back row: Willingham (Huddersfield), Broome (Aston Villa), Lawton (Everton), Davies (trainer), Woodley (Chelsea), Gardiner (Wolves), Mercer (Everton), Greenhalgh (Everton). Front row: Matthews (Stoke), Hall (Spurs), Cullis (Wolves), Sproston (Spurs), Dix (Derby), Boyes (WBA). It was his fine performance in this match that brought Ronnie Dix his England cap against Norway a week later. He joined Spurs in 1939.

Johnny Morrison misses an open goal opportunity in the home match against Luton Town on Saturday 29 January 1938. He made amends later by actually scoring, to which Colin Lyman added two more goals for a Spurs victory. Morrison was the top scorer in 1937/38 with 25 goals.

Having entertained Germany in 1935, international football came to White Hart Lane again on Wednesday 1 December 1937, when England were hosts to Czechoslovakia. Playing for England at inside right was Willie Hall, who had won his first England cap on the same ground in 1933 against France.

Tottenham's goalkeeper, Percy Hooper, makes a save in a match against Chesterfield in 1938. Hooper had eleven seasons at Tottenham, which were bisected by the war. He was a reserve goalkeeper with Islington Corinthians when he joined Spurs in April 1935. He played 245 games for the club before moving on in 1947 to Swansea for one year, then Southern League Chingford. He finished his career with Kings Lynn.

Action from the Spurs *v.* Blackburn Rovers FA Cup third round match at White Hart Lane in 1938. A 3-2 win saw Spurs progress, but they needed replays in the next two rounds to dispose of New Brighton and Chesterfield. Eventually they went out of the competition in the sixth round, losing 1-0 to Sunderland in front of their record attendance of 75,038.

Colin Lyman scores Spurs' equalizing goal against Norwich City on 1 October 1938. Tottenham went on to win the match 4-1. The other Spurs player is Albert Hall. Before the kick-off, both teams had lined up for the National Anthem as an act of thanksgiving that war had been averted.

Tottenham Hotspur FC, 1938/39. From left to right, back row: McCormick, Sproston, Page, Hooper, Buckingham, Spelman. Front row: Whatley, Sargent, W. Hall, Morrison, A. Hall, Lyman. Peter McWilliam returned to manage Spurs and promptly gave some youngsters their chance. Bill Nicholson made his debut at Blackburn in October and Ron Burgess first appeared in February at Norwich, both players having come through the nursery at Northfleet. Bert Sproston was signed from Leeds United, but then announced that he could not settle in London, and moved to Manchester City after only ten matches in Spurs colours. Signing for the City on Friday 4 November, he played against Tottenham the next day at Maine Road. He was selected for England while on Spurs' books. This was the season that Willie Hall set up a record by scoring five goals for England v. Ireland at Old Trafford in November 1938 – this feat was even more remarkable as Hall was not really renowned for his goalscoring powers! The season had started well in a Jubilee Trust Fund game, when Arsenal, the current League Champions, were beaten 2-0 at Highbury, Spurs' goals coming from Morrison and Lyman. The leading scorers this season were Morrison and W. Hall with 11 goals apiece. The FA Cup final came close to being played at White Hart Lane in this season and was earmarked for the replay if the tie had not been settled at Wembley.

It took three meetings between Tottenham and West Ham to decide who progressed to the next round of the FA Cup in February 1939. This is part of the action in the third game at Highbury, the white-shirted Tottenham players being Fred Sargent (on the ground), and Albert Hall. West Ham won through after the three games had brought in an aggregate attendance of 143,982.

The numbering of players' shirts came about mainly through Tottenham's regular suggestions at meetings of the League clubs during the late 1930s. The idea was finally taken up just before the war and Spurs paraded numbers on their backs for the FA Cup-tie against Watford in January 1939. It was at this time that this photograph, showing Andy Duncan, Albert Hall and Willie Hall admiring their newly modified attire ready for the match, was taken.

Four

The War Years and After

Johnny Morrison, a prolific scorer for Spurs just before the war, is seen here netting versus West Bromwich Albion at White Hart Lane in January 1939. Morrison was the kind of centre forward who, despite a lack of skill, always seemed to be in the right place at the right time, often missing easy chances and scoring with remarkable efforts. His final Spurs record was an impressive 132 goals in 190 matches.

A.H. 'Jack' Gibbons, Tottenham's top scorer during the war years. The renowned amateur centre forward had one season with Tottenham in 1937/38, but then decided to play for Brentford. He rejoined Tottenham in 1939 and then played throughout the war, scoring 89 goals. These included four hat-tricks on successive Saturdays, all against Clapton Orient. A constant member of the England amateur side, he also played for the full England side in October 1942 versus Wales. His overall record for Spurs was 109 goals from 148 appearances.

Jimmy McCormick joined Tottenham from Chesterfield in 1932. He was a speedy little winger who reminded older Spurs fans of the immortal Fanny Walden. Like many others, his career was split by the war and he guested for fourteen different clubs in this period. He left for Fulham in 1946 and went on to have a spell at Lincoln City before coaching in Malta and Turkey. He was killed in a car accident in January 1969, when on holiday in Spain.

Born in Islington, Fred Sargent moved through the usual ranks at Tottenham, and their nursery club Northfleet, and was offered professional terms in 1934. He was a regular on the right wing up until the war, and when peace came the thirty-three year old Fred moved to Chelmsford to play out his career. Sadly, he died only two years later.

FREDDIE
COX

Spotted by Tottenham when just a lad, Freddie Cox made his Spurs debut at the age of eighteen against Swansea Town in November 1938, scoring twice. A fast moving and sometimes acrobatic winger, Freddie was in the RAF during the war and was awarded the Distinguished Flying Cross. Losing his team spot in 1949, he joined Arsenal for £12,000. Later, he became manager at Bournemouth, Portsmouth and Gillingham.

The programme for the 12 August 1939 practice match at White Hart Lane, between the Whites and the Stripes, gave no indication that after only three League matches the outbreak of war would change everything. The numbering of the players also started properly during this abortive season, the programme showing each team as 1 to 11 (formerly the line-ups were printed as 1 to 22).

At inside left for the Whites in the practice match was Ronnie Dix, Spurs' new signing from Derby County, who had cost the club £8,000. He had made his name with Bristol Rovers, playing in their first team at the age of only fifteen, before moving on to Blackburn Rovers, Aston Villa and then Derby. He scored in his only appearance for England *v.* Norway, which England won 4-0. He played very few times for Spurs through the war, being stationed near Blackpool, where he became a regular member of their wartime side, playing for them in the Football League North Cup finals in 1943 and 1944. When the League was restarted after the war, Ronnie was nearing the end of his playing career and, after one-and-a-half seasons at White Hart Lane, he moved to Reading before finally retiring in 1949.

George Ludford was another Tottenham player who turned out for a different club in a Wartime Cup final. He is pictured here, just to the right of King George VI, as the Millwall team, of which he was a member, was introduced to His Majesty before the game. The Lions lost 2-0 to Chelsea in this 1945 final tie, which was played at Wembley.

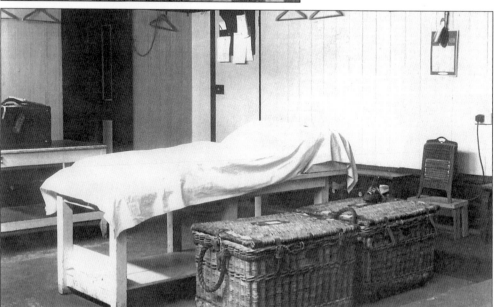

Not quite the luxury of years to come, this view of the White Hart Lane dressing rooms from the early 1940s shows that they were pretty basic. Note the ancient portable electric fire, boarded walls, wooden coat hangers and the treatment table in the centre of the room.

Football programmes suffered from the paper shortage in the war, most teams, including Spurs, cutting them down to a single sheet – indeed, this Reading team sheet was printed on only one side. The Spurs team, showing three changes from the side printed here, won this match 6-2. Reading were a man short so Spurs let them borrow their reserve Billy Sainsbury. Tottenham had to be ferried to the ground from the railway station by private cars when travel arrangements broke down.

ELM PARK

SATURDAY, OCTOBER 17th, 1942.

Football League South.

TOTTENHAM

Right Wing   *Left Wing*

HOME TEAM

An N Other
Penny.

2—Goldberg   3—Fullwood

4—Aicken   5—Milligan   6—Cothliffe

7—Chitty   8—M. Edelston   9—McPhee   10—Bradley   11—Painter

11—Ludford 10—O'Callaghan 9—A. H. Gibbons 8—Martin 7—Beasley

6—Hall   5—J. Chisholm   4—R. White

3—Whatley   2—Ward

Ditchburn

T OTTENHAM.

Left Wing   *Right Wing*

Referee—A. WALTER.
Linesmen—Messrs. T. BOWER and V. BULL

NEXT HOME MATCH—
BERKS & BUCKS SENIOR CUP—(1st Round)

RESERVES v. **R.A.F.T.C.** (H.Q.)

OCTOBER 24th.   KICK-OFF 3-15.

Official Team Sheet—ONE PENNY.

It was in the 1942/43 season that the sprightly figure of Group Captain Donald Finlay, the Great Britain Olympic hurdler, was seen on Tottenham's right wing, for three matches. He thrilled everyone with his amateur style of wing play, as he used his great speed to dash goalwards, although well into his thirties by this time.

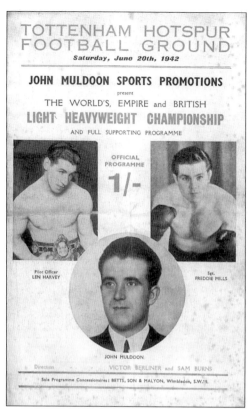

On Saturday 20 June 1942, boxing came to White Hart Lane when Pilot Officer Len Harvey was opposed by Sgt Freddie Mills for the World, Empire and British Light Heavyweight Championship, which Mills won with a knockout in the second round. Ringside seats for this event were £5 5s 0d – quite a sizable portion of most people's wages at the time! In a supporting bout was a young heavyweight named Bruce Woodcock, who came back to the White Hart Lane arena in 1945 to win the Heavyweight Championship of Great Britain.

The RAF team of 1943 was one of the best to be put out by the service. From left to right back row: Franklin, Soo, Hayward, Scott, Marks, Hardwick, Ron Burgess (Tottenham Hotspur), Squadron Leader Tom Whittaker. Front row: Matthews, Carter, Drake, Mortensen, Smith.

A photograph taken from the terrace of the two Tottenham sides leaving the field after a 1943 pre-season practice match at White Hart Lane. Ralph Ward is seen leading the players towards the dressing rooms. The upper tier of the east stand was not being used at this time. It had been used at the start of the war as a temporary morgue during the heavy air raids over the district.

When Tottenham signed Colin Lyman from Northampton in 1937 he went straight into the first team, playing regularly for two seasons. During the war he was much in demand as a guest and, being stationed mainly in the Midlands, he played for Derby County, Chesterfield, Northampton, Leicester and Coventry amongst others. In 1946 he left Spurs and settled in Nottingham.

Vic Buckingham wore the Tottenham shirt with pride for fourteen seasons, making 311 appearances. He came through the usual Spurs ranks and made his debut in 1935 versus Bury. He found himself playing against Spurs during the war as he guested for other clubs, but only after making great efforts to reach White Hart Lane from wherever he was stationed. He also appeared twice for the England team against Wales. He had a fine career after playing, coaching and then managing various clubs, including Ajax, Bradford and West Bromwich Albion.

Tottenham, along with most clubs, managed to produce a match programme throughout the war years, and this single-sheet publication, produced for a 1944 game against Millwall, also shows the ranks of the Spurs players in the Forces. Directions to the nearest air raid shelters in case of an emergency are also included. This is quite an unusual programme as the Spurs team played as printed – a rare feat in those turbulent days.

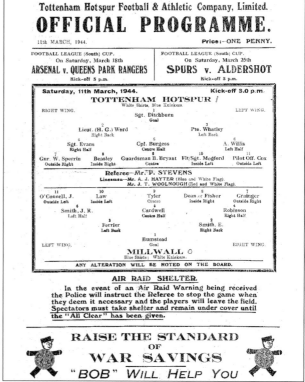

The 1943/44 and 1944/45 seasons were two of Tottenham's most successful campaigns, as they won the championship of the Football League South in both of them. Shown here are the main players who helped to achieve this. From left to right, back row: Sonny Walters, George Ludford, Ralph Ward, Archie Hughes, Arthur Willis, Roy White. Middle row: George Hardy (trainer), Pat Beasley, Charlie Burke, Albert Hall, Jack Chisholm, Les Medley, Les Stevens, Jimmy Anderson (coach), Will Over (groundsman). Front row: W. Heryet, F. Wale, E. Dewhurst-Hornsby (directors), Fred Bearman (chairman), G. Cox (director), Arthur Turner (secretary-manager). The wartime experiences of two of these players are particularly interesting. Roy White had been blinded for a while when coming off the Dunkirk beaches, while Albert Hall had been a Japanese POW before escaping when his prisoner transport was sunk – he spent several hours in the sea before being rescued and was one of only a few survivors. He had a special cheer when he appeared for his comeback game at White Hart Lane. Often during the 1943/44 season, the Spurs paraded an all-guest forward line of Beasley (Huddersfield), Martin (Aston Villa), Rowley (Manchester United), O'Donnell (Aston Villa) and Jones (West Bromwich Albion).

G.W. 'Willie' Hall was one of the most popular players to wear a Tottenham shirt, captaining the team on many occasions. He was signed from Notts County in 1932 and made his debut for Spurs against his old team almost straightaway, pulling the strings as his new side gained promotion. His talent was soon rewarded when he was picked for England in 1933 and scored 9 goals in 10 internationals, including five in one match against Ireland in 1938. He played in many positions during the war for Spurs as, like most clubs, they struggled to put eleven players out each week. It was in 1943 that a serious disease forced him to retire and resulted in his having both lower legs amputated. After trying to be a manager for a short time, he took over a public house for some years. Willie died in 1967.

At the end of the 1945/46 season, Tottenham played a benefit match for Willie Hall. Their opponents were a strong Football Association XI containing some current international players. Numerous players contacted the club wishing to take part in this match. Willie greeted each player as they entered the field and then sat back to watch his old Spurs team-mates win 4-1.

OFFICIAL PROGRAMME.

Tottenham Hotspur Football & Athletic Company, Limited.

CHAIRMAN:—F. J. Bearman.

Directors:—M. F. CADMAN, GEORGE COX. G. WAGSTAFFE SIMMONS. F.J.I.,
W. J. HERVET, R. DEWHURST HORNSBY, FREDk. WALE.

SECRETARY:—A. W. Turner.

7b MAY, 1946.   Price:—ONE PENNY.

FINAL, SUN SHIELD.

On Monday, May 13th.

EDMONTON BOYS

v.

WEST HAM BOYS or S. LONDON BOYS

Kick-off 6.30 p.m.

G. W. HALL Benefit Match. Tues., May 7th, 1946. Kick-off 6.30 p.m.

TOTTENHAM HOTSPUR

White Shirts. Blue Knickers.

RIGHT WING.   LEFT WING

1
Ditchburn
Goal

2   3
Willis   Buckingham
Right Back   Left Back

4   5   6
Ludford   Nicholson   Burgess (Capt.)
Right Half   Centre Half   Left Half

7   8   9   10   11
Cox   Bennett   Foreman   A. H. Gibbons   Medley
Outside Right   Inside Right   Centre   Inside Left   Outside Left

Referee Mr. A. T. FORD (Essex).

Linesmen—Mr. G. HORNETT (Middx.) (Blue and White Flag).
Mr. J. B. RITTELL (London) (Red and White Flag).

11   10   9   8   7
Hancocks (Walsall)   Drury (Arsenal)   Stubbins (New. U.)   Wainwright (Everton)   Roper (Saints)
Outside Left   Inside Left   Centre   Inside Right   Outside Right

6   5   4
Mitchell (Birm.)   Smith (Brentford)   Machent (Sheff. Utd.)
Left Half   Centre Half   Right Half

3   2
Robinson (Middlesbrough)   McCue (Stoke)
Left Back   Right Back

1
Williams (Wolves)
Goal

LEFT WING.   RIGHT WING.

F.A. ELEVEN

Blue Shirts. White Knickers.

ANY ALTERATION WILL BE NOTED ON THE BOARD.

TOTTENHAM'S FINE FINISH

We concluded our League South programme at Coventry with a win, Foreman scoring the only goal of the game, in the second half. We are ninth in the programme, and what a change has come over the scene. This can best be shown by a comparison of the results of the first ten and the last ten games in the League:—

	W	D	L	F	A	Pts.
First Ten	2	1	7	18	34	5
Last Ten	9	0	1	17	4	18

Those figures are very encouraging for next season, when we shall be fighting in the Second Division to gain promotion.

It was our intention to present a complete set of statistics covering every aspect of the season now ended, but paper shortage will not permit of this. The Directors express sincere thanks to the thousands of loyal supporters for their attendance at our games, and on your behalf to the players for the way in which they recovered from a disheartening start, and the glorious finish they provided for us. And now, Good-bye until August.

The crowd is gathered in front of the old west stand to see the League South Cup being presented to Spurs in 1945. The actual trophy can be seen at the extreme bottom left of the picture. The supporters were then beginning to swarm back to the matches as the war was coming to its conclusion.

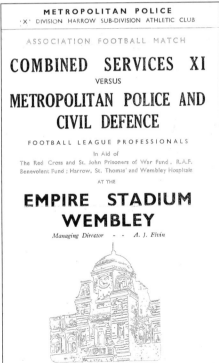

METROPOLITAN POLICE
'X' DIVISION HARROW SUB-DIVISION ATHLETIC CLUB

ASSOCIATION FOOTBALL MATCH

COMBINED SERVICES XI

VERSUS

METROPOLITAN POLICE AND CIVIL DEFENCE

FOOTBALL LEAGUE PROFESSIONALS

In Aid of
The Red Cross and St. John Prisoners of War Fund, R.A.F.
Benevolent Fund ; Harrow, St. Thomas' and Wembley Hospitals

AT THE

EMPIRE STADIUM WEMBLEY

Managing Director - - A. J. Elvin

Wednesday, May 10th, 1944, kick off 7 p.m.

OFFICIAL PROGRAMME - SIXPENCE

The programme for the Wembley meeting between the Combined Services XI and the Metropolitan Police and Civil Defence XI in 1944. This was one of the many representative games arranged to raise money for the war effort. There were five current Spurs players involved in this match and another (Foreman) who joined the club later on.

107

F. McEWAN.   Inside-left.
Height 5ft. 9½in.   Weight 11st 6lbs.
Born at Airdrie.
Played for Airdrienians.

One of the new Tottenham players signed just before the war was Frank McEwan who came from Scottish club Airdrieonians. He became an ambulance driver at Edmonton and, after playing three matches for Spurs, was called up and drafted abroad. McEwan was killed in action in September 1944.

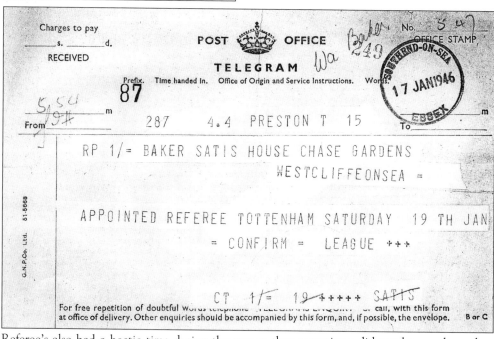

Referee's also had a hectic time during the war as they sometimes did not know where they would be sent, although they were promised that their journeys would be kept short – this was a promise that was not often kept. This telegram shows that only two days notice was given for this referee to take charge at White Hart Lane for the game versus Luton Town on Saturday 19 January 1946.

The Tottenham line-up for the first 'proper' post-war season of 1946/47. From left to right, back row: Bennett, Buckingham, Page, Hughes, Ditchburn, Chisholm, Woodward, Nicholson, Dorling. Third row: Hardy (trainer), Skinner, Tickridge, Foreman, Hiscoke, Lown, Duquemin, Poynton (assistant trainer), J. Coxford. Second row: Trailor, Gilberg, Dix, Burgess, Ludford, Rundle, Whatley. Front row: Cox, Griffiths, Stevens, A. Hall, Willis. Tottenham found it a bit hard going as they started in Division Two once more, opening their season with a home game against Birmimgham City and going down 2-1, with George Foreman getting the Spurs goal. Les Bennett was back from the Forces and became top scorer with 19 goals. Ronnie Dix was starting all over again from the 1939 season, but was no longer the force that persuaded Spurs to sign him six years previously, and he soon moved on to Reading. Walters and Baily were beginning to appear on the horizon, but were still serving their country. No new signings were made as the club relied on their own home-produced resources. The aggregate attendance for the twenty home games was 751,519 – not too bad for a Division Two side – but the target of promotion was not achieved, although twenty-four players were used to try to get the right combination. The club went on an end-of-season tour to the south of France, where they won two and lost two of their four matches. During this season the colour of the programmes was changed from salmon to white.

Tottenham Hotspur FC, 1947/48. From left to right, back row: Nicholson, Trailor, J. Hulme (manager), Tickridge, Ditchburn, Woodward, Burgess, Buckingham. Front row: Ludford, Cox, Jordan, Duquemin, Baily, E. Jones, Bennett. This was a season that promised much and included a fine FA Cup run through to the semi-finals, but after going out of the competition they won only two more matches in the run-in for promotion. In fact, Spurs failed to score in eight of these games and slipped out of the title race. The biggest crowd at White Hart Lane was 71,835 for the FA Cup-tie against West Bromwich Albion. Representative honours came to some players during the season: Ron Burgess captained Wales, Bill Nicholson played for England 'B', Ted Ditchburn was in goal for the Football League and a Football Association XI, Charlie Withers and Harry Gilberg both played in Brussels for the Football Combination XI, while Sonny Walters appeared for the British Army team. It was left to the reserves to bring some silverware to White Hart Lane, winning the London Challenge Cup by beating Fulham 3-1. At the season's end, Spurs visited the Channel Islands for two matches, in which Len Duquemin captained the Tottenham side against his fellow islanders.

Len Duquemin, seen here in action against West Bromwich Albion in the FA Cup, scored eight goals in the cup matches of 1948, including a hat-trick in the victory over Leicester City. A true clubman, the 'Duke' ranks amongst the best of Spurs' goalscorers, and could have become the first Channel Islander to play for England.

The FA Cup run created tremendous interest as Spurs reached the semis for the first time since 1922. Bolton Wanderers were beaten 2-0 away, West Bromwich at home 3-1, Leicester at home 5-2 and Southampton at the Dell 1-0. Then came the dramatic semi-final against Blackpool at Villa Park. Spurs were leading 1-0 with four minutes left when Mortensen equalized and then netted two more during extra time. The picture shows one of Mortensen's goals as he lobs the ball over Ditchburn. The other Tottenham players in the photograph are Tickridge (2) and Nicholson.

JOHNNY JORDAN
(Tottenham Hotspur)

Johnny Jordan spent only one season with Tottenham (1947/48) and scored 13 goals in 27 games. Born in Romford, he had been an amateur at Grays Athletic and was even selected as a reserve for the England Amateurs. When Spurs signed him as a professional, they put him straight into the first eleven. He became one of the first British players to go to Italy when Juventus made Spurs a big offer for his services but, like so many others that followed, he failed to settle and returned to England and Birmingham City.

Ted Ditchburn, a son of a boxer, was arguably the best-ever Tottenham goalkeeper. He progressed through the Northfleet nursery and made his first appearance for Spurs in the wartime side. Ditchburn was selected for England *v*. Scotland in 1944.

Ron Burgess came to White Hart Lane in 1936. In his early days he played in the forward line and was amongst the goals. However, a year later when Spurs were thinking of releasing him, he filled the wing half position at the last minute for the 'A' team. This changed the club's mind, and he stayed for another seventeen years. The war years saw Ron at centre forward on many occasions as well as at half-back, and he played his first game for Wales *v.* England on 11 November 1939. He became captain of Tottenham after the war, leading the side to promotion from Division Two and the Championship of Division One in successive seasons.

RON BURGESS (SPURS)

One of the biggest crowds of the 1947/48 season was at White Hart Lane for the visit of the eventual champions Birmingham City on 13 December 1947. This action shot shows two Tottenham defenders, Vic Buckingham (3) and Horace Woodward, trying to prevent a Birmingham shot at the home goal. A crowd of 53,730 saw this match, which Spurs lost narrowly by the odd goal in three.

TOTTENHAM HOTSPURS FINE CENTRE FORWARD

Len Duquemin alias "THE DUKE"

THE CHANNEL ISLANDER WHOSE SPORTING AND UNSELFISH PLAY, MAKE HIM A FIRM FAVOURITE WHEREVER HE GOES.

Len is good with his head, can dribble, and has a terrific shot —

Len Duquemin became an instant favourite with Spurs supporters, making his debut in March 1946 at Fulham. He had turned up for a trial before being rapidly signed and farmed out to Chelmsford City, managed by Arthur Rowe at the time. Len led the Tottenham attack with success through the late 1940s and early '50s, putting in his workmanlike performances, week after week, for thirteen seasons. When he left the club in 1958, he had made 374 appearances and scored 184 goals. He had spells with Bedford Town, Hastings and Romford before settling down to run his newsagents shop, later becoming a landlord at Cheshunt.

The board of directors of Tottenham Hotspur Football Club in 1948. From left to right, back row: F. Wale, G. Wagstaff Simmons, A.W. Turner (secretary), E. Dewhurst-Hornsby, W.J. Heyret. Front row: G. Cox, F.J. Bearman (chairman), M. Cadman. Arthur Turner was at the helm throughout the war years and put in a lot of sterling work. Mr Morton Cadman had served the longest, being elected to the board in 1900. He had played in his younger days and been a member of the committee when the club was an amateur organisation. Mr Wagstaff Simmons put together the first comprehensive history of the club that was published in 1947.

In eight seasons following the war, Ted Ditchburn missed only two matches for Tottenham and, from April 1948, played in 247 consecutive games, appearing for England 6 times. Spurs fans heaved a sigh of relief each week when they saw Ted following his captain out of the tunnel for Tottenham.

Tottenham had turned to an ex-Arsenal man to take them forward when the war finished, but when they failed to gain promotion Joe Hulme resigned. Here, the ex-winger is pictured trying to show Burgess how to tackle.

Sid Tickridge was yet another player who came through the Spurs youth scheme at this time. He made his debut during the war, having been with Dartford and Tottenham Juniors. A regular before being called into the Navy, he lost his place to Alf Ramsey and left Spurs after ten years, moving to Chelsea and Brentford before returning to the Tottenham fold later as youth team trainer.

TOTTENHAM HOTSPUR
FOOTBALL AND ATHLETIC COMPANY, LIMITED

OFFICIAL PROGRAMME
AND RECORD OF THE CLUB

ISSUED EVERY **MATCH DAY**	Chairman : FRED J. BEARMAN Directors : GEORGE COX, W. J. HERYET, E. DEWHURST HORNSB'', Rt. Hon. Lord MORRISON, G. WAGSTAFFE SIMMONS, F.J.I., FREDK. WALE Secretary : A. W. TURNER Team Manager : J. H. A. HULME	**PRICE** **TWOPENCE**

VOL. XLI. No. 40   MARCH 5th. 1949

A DRAW AND TWO WINS

The point we obtained at Blackburn last Saturday was of priceless value. Positions in the League table depend not only upon what any particular club does, but also how their immediate rivals fare. This fact was dramatically emphasised last week-end.

Before the games were played the Spurs were fourth, West Bromwich Albion being second a point ahead, and Fulham level with us on points but with a slightly superior goal average. Southampton, who have been showing consistently good form of late, were at the head, and they strengthened their hold on the topmost rung of the ladder with a comfortable win over Barnsley at The Dell.

It was generally expected that Fulham, who had been scoring so freely, would credit themselves with a win at Shepherd's Bush over Queen's Park Rangers, who had not had a League win since Boxing Day, when they won in West London over Blackburn Rovers 4—2. The Rangers took the lead in the first half against Fulham, and clung

OUR FOOTBALL QUIZ

(Answers on next page)

1. What ranks as the record for the greatest distance any player was away from England when he signed for a Football League club ?
2. Which clubs supply the two instances of neighbouring teams having been drawn together most times in the F.A. Cup ?
3. Which famous player appeared in international football when he was not associated with any club and was disengaged ?
4. How many players in history have figured in an Irish Cup-winning team and an F.A. Cup-winning side in successive seasons ?
5. Which famous English international forward played his first match on first joining a Football League club against German opposition and ended his career by coaching Germans ?
6. Which is the only Football League club whose existing ground record attendance was created when, as a First Division team, it was playing a Third Division side ?

THE ENFIELD CENTRAL BAND WILL PLAY AT EACH HOME GAME

Printed by Thomas Knight & Co., Ltd., The Clock House Press, Hoddesdon, Herts.

The size and shape of the Tottenham programme was the same from its inception when the club entered the Football League until 1961, the only change being the colour. The cartoon fronts disappeared in 1946, as this cover for the game against Cardiff City in March 1949 shows.

To make sure of getting into White Hart Lane often meant a long wait in a queue, sometimes of two hours or more. This photograph, taken in 1949, shows a line of supporters stretching across a street, herded by relaxed policemen, including one on a white horse. Note the bicycles leaning against the rather unsafe garden fence (and possibly still there for their owners after the match).

Supporters rush to get to their favourite positions as the gates are opened for a 1949 match. Even those who preferred standing on the terraces had their favoured places and woe betide anyone who stood in their spot. In the late 1940s the gates had to be closed at numerous games before kick-off time for safety reasons, and people were turned away from the ground.

Tottenham Hotspur FC, 1948/49. From left to right, back row: Bennett, Burgess, Markham, Ditchburn, Hodge, Duquemin, Heseltine. Third row: Joe Hulme, Robshaw, Williams, Ludford, Garwood, E. Jones, Trailor, Tickridge, Nicholson, Gibbons, Woodward, Buckingham, Toulouse, Cecil Poynton. Second row: Cox, Willis, Henty, Gilberg, Withers, Foreman, Medley, Walters, Sullivan, Stevens, Flint. Front row: Rundle, Westwood, Harmer, Baily, Scarth, Elmes, Wallis. After topping the table in October and still in second place as late as February, Spurs missed out yet again on promotion. One factor was possibly the death of Arthur Turner, who had given outstanding service to the club since 1906. Two attendances of over 69,000 were recorded for the home games against Queens Park Rangers and Southampton. The only players to appear in every match for this season were Ted Ditchburn and Les Bennett; Ditchburn also made his first full England appearance against Switzerland at Highbury. One of the biggest upsets was when bottom club Lincoln City won 2-1 at White Hart Lane on New Years Day, with ex-Spur Jimmy McCormick in their side. Two significant events took place towards the end of the season: Harry Clarke signed from Lovells Athletic and Arthur Rowe took over as manager from Joe Hulme.

Even in the summer break Tottenham players were good for an interesting picture. Here, at Butlins Holiday Camp in 1948, are the notable Taylor Quads being shown off by Les Bennett, Ron Burgess, Ernie Jones and Ted Ditchburn.

Arthur Rowe served Tottenham well over the years, first as a player and then as manager. He was born within a short distance of the Spurs' ground, made his first appearance for the senior team in October 1931 and soon became the permanent centre half. He returned as manager in 1949 with his 'push and run' style of playing the game, which proved a great success in Tottenham's successive championship years of 1950 and 1951.

White Hart Lane was chosen for the England v. Italy international match in 1949, with new Spurs signing Alf Ramsey occupying the right-back position for England, who won 2-0.

THE FOOTBALL ASSOCIATION

INTERNATIONAL MATCH

ENGLAND
v.
ITALY

On TOTTENHAM HOTSPUR
GROUND, HIGH ROAD
TOTTENHAM, N.17

Wednesday, November 30th
1949

KICK-OFF 2.15 p.m.

PROGRAMME SIXPENCE

Action from the England v. Italy match showing Ramsey stopping a shot, while goalkeeper Bert Williams struggles to get across his goal to save.

After his arrival as manager, Arthur Rowe lost no time in getting to know his team. Here he is, with trainer Cecil Poynton on the left, holding a tactical talk with the Spurs players. From left to right, back row: Harry Clarke, Ron Burgess, Billy Rees, Les Medley, Les Bennett, Bill Nicholson, Alf Ramsey. Front row: Charlie Withers, Eddie Baily, Sonny Walters, Ted Ditchburn.

Alf Ramsey, seen here in England's colours, was always the cool head in Tottenham's defence after joining from Southampton. Dagenham-born Ramsey was twenty-nine when he moved to Tottenham for £21,000 and was already an international. He was also the intelligent penalty taker for the side, relying on a well-placed shot rather than a powerful drive. The last link in manager Rowe's renowned side, he developed a great understanding with goalkeeper Ditchburn, often picking up his short throws out of defence.

TOTTENHAM HOTSPUR

FOOTBALL AND ATHLETIC COMPANY, LIMITED

Souvenir Programme

This programme has been issued by the Directors—on the occasion of the visit of Grimsby Town for the last home league match of the season—as a tribute to the Tottenham players on winning the Championship of Division II of the Football League and Promotion to the First Division.

Secretary: R. S. JARVIS

Team Manager: ARTHUR S. ROWE

Medical Officer: Dr. A. E. TUGHAN

President: The Right Hon. LORD MORRISON, P.C., D.L., J.P.

Chairman: FRED J. BEARMAN

Directors: GEORGE COX, W. J. HERYET, E. DEWHURST HORNSBY, G. WAGSTAFFE SIMMONS, F.J.I., HARRY TAYLOR, FREDK. WALE

PRICE

TWOPENCE

VOL. XLII. No. 60.   SATURDAY, APRIL 22nd, 1950

A Message from the President

Before this unforgettable season closes I want publicly to thank the Boys for winning promotion to the First Division after a fifteen years' break.

Ever since last August they have been playing the kind of football that delights the heart of every lover of the game.

It has frequently been my privilege to accompany them on their travels, and a better bunch of fellows than Ron Burgess and his merry men I never expect to meet.

Congratulations also to Arthur Rowe for a fine job of work in his first year as Manager.

If space permitted I should like to mention several others who have helped, but one more must suffice—Cecil Poynton, the man with the magic sponge, who has kept the boys fighting fit for their strenuous task.

Now, what about next season? Well! your guess is as good as mine, and here's mine:—

First class football played in the best traditions of our famous club.

TOTTENHAM HOTSPUR F.C.—FIRST TEAM, 1949–50

Back Row (left to right): A. RAMSEY, W. REES, L. BENNETT, E. DITCHBURN, H. CLARKE, R. BURGESS, C. WITHERS.
Front Row (left to right): W. NICHOLSON, G. LUDFORD, W. WALTERS, J. SCARTH, L. DUQUEMIN, E. BAILY, L. MEDLEY.

Tottenham celebrated winning the Division Two championship with an illustrated programme for their last home game against Grimsby Town on 22 April 1950, after which the trophy was presented to the club. However, the visitors somewhat spoilt the party by winning 2-1. Only eighteen players were needed to secure the title for Spurs, but Cook only played three times, Willis and Marchi twice, Scarth and Ludford four times, and Tickridge once. This demonstrates the adage that a settled side is a successful one.

TOTTENHAM HOTSPUR

FOOTBALL AND ATHLETIC COMPANY, LIMITED

President: The Right Hon. LORD MORRISON, P.C., D.L., J.P.

Official Programme

AND RECORD OF THE CLUB

Secretary: R. S. JARVIS

Team Manager:
ARTHUR S. ROWE
Medical Officers:
Dr. A. E. TUGHAN

Chairman: FRED J. BEARMAN
Directors: F. JOHN BEARMAN, Wm. J. HERYET,
E. DEWHURST HORNSBY, G. WAGSTAFFE SIMPSONS, F.J.I.,
HARRY TAYLOR, FREDK. WALE

PRICE
TWOPENCE

VOL. XLIII. No. 52.   SATURDAY, MAY 5th, 1951

SOMETHING TO CROW ABOUT

OUR BOYS. DO IT AGAIN!

FOR A WONDERFUL SEASON WE SAY TO YOU ALL

WELL DONE AND THANK YOU!

THE ENFIELD CENTRAL BAND WILL PLAY AT EACH HOME GAME

Printed by Thomas Knight & Co. Ltd., The Clock House Press, Hoddesdon, Herts.

There was another small change to the programme for the last match of the Division One championship season, which was against Liverpool. A well-drawn caricature cover featuring the Spurs team with their manager. In this season's final match, Peter Murphy scored twice and Walters once to seal a 3-1 victory.

Les Bennett rises high for a goal attempt, watched by Duquemin and Murphy during a 1-0 victory over Manchester United at White Hart Lane, a Walters goal securing the points. The fine lines of the east stand are shown beautifully in this photograph.

A historic picture showing the Football League Championship trophy being presented to Spurs captain Ron Burgess by the Football League president Arthur Drewry. This was the first time in their long history that Tottenham had managed to become Football League champions, finishing four points ahead of runners-up Manchester United.

After two Festival of Britain matches in early May, Spurs embarked on a short tour to Denmark. Here, the party are boarding their aircraft prior to the outward flight. From left to right: Nicholson, Medley, Duquemin, Walters, Poynton (trainer), Ditchburn and Willis.

Tottenham Hotspur FC, 1951/52. They are shown with the League trophy that they had won the previous season. From left to right, back row: A. Rowe (manager), Ramsey, Withers, McClellan, Uphill, Poynton (trainer), Dr A. Tughan (medical officer). Third row: H. Taylor (director), Brittan, Duquemin, Ditchburn, E. Dewhurst-Hornsby (director), Clarke, Bennett, R. Jarvis (secretary). Second row: F. Wale (director), Right Hon. Lord Morrison (president), Nicholson, F. Bearman (chairman), Burgess, G. Wagstaff Simmons (director), W. Heryet (director). Front row: Medley, Willis, Baily, Walters. After a home defeat by Arsenal on 9 February, Spurs did not taste defeat in any more of their League games and moved swiftly up the Division One table to finish in second spot. Tommy 'The Charmer' Harmer made his League debut during this campaign against Bolton Wanderers in September 1951, while Brian Farley, who had been with the club since 1949, made his one and only appearance in the opening game of the season against Middlesbrough. Uproar followed Spurs' home match with Huddersfield, who were fighting against dropping out of the top flight, when Spurs won with a disputed goal – Baily's corner kick rebounded to him off the referee before he crossed again for Duquemin to head home the winner – as a result of which Huddersfield were relegated.

In March 1952 Tottenham Hotspur took time out from the League programme to travel to Brussels for a friendly against FC Austria, which they drew 2-2, Bennett and Duquemin being the marksmen. The top picture shows the Spurs team in the dressing room before the game, while the bottom one shows some of the Tottenham players relaxing in the lounge at Brussels airport before flying home.

HE ALSO SERVES WHO ONLY SITS AND WAITS.

This cartoon appeared in the Tottenham Hotspur Christmas programme in 1950, showing manager Arthur Rowe dreaming of the 'double' of FA Cup and Football League Championship. He was, however, about ten years too early in his happy thoughts!